A HAUNT OF RARE SOULS

'...*there is nothing which has yet been contrived by man, by which so much happiness is produced, as by a good tavern or inn.*'

Doctor Johnson

A HAUNT OF
RARE SOULS

The Old Inns and Pubs of Yorkshire

Barrie Pepper

Foreword by Malcolm Barker

SMITH SETTLE

First published in 1990 by

Smith Settle Ltd
Ilkley Road
Otley
West Yorkshire
LS21 3JP

ISBN Paperback 1 870071 46 8
Hardback 1 870071 47 6

British Library Cataloguing in Publication Data
Pepper, Barrie
    A haunt of rare souls: the old inns and pubs of Yorkshire.
    1. Yorkshire. Public houses
    I. Title
    647.954281

ISBN 1-870071-47-6
ISBN 1-870071-46-8 pbk

Designed, printed and bound by
SMITH SETTLE
Ilkley Road, Otley, West Yorkshire LS21 3JP

To David — boon companion.

'Will someone take me to a pub?'

G K Chesterton

CONTENTS

ILLUSTRATIONS

PHOTOGRAPHIC ACKNOWLEDGEMENTS

For permission to reproduce the undermentioned illustrations, thanks are due to the following:

David Atkinson, p55; Bass (North) Ltd, p6, 32, 34, 70 (top), 96 (top/bottom), 139, 149, 165, 186; Black Swan, Helmsley, p162; Gary Firth, p67, 73 (bottom); Mr and Mrs R Goodall, p160; Malcolm Greenwood, p25; Milford Harrison, p187; Stephen Kavanagh, p57; Mrs Irene Law, p52; Leeds Libraries, p44; Barry Moy, p8; MTD Rigg Publications, p204; Malcolm G Neesam, p212; North Yorkshire County Libraries, p171; Michael Philbin, p30; Peter Robinson, p78, 81, 83; Benny Smith, p8, 26, 180; Timothy Taylor & Co Ltd, p223; Joshua Tetley & Co Ltd, p41, 43, 218, and John Broadley's drawings, p68, 79, 97, 107, 112, 176; Thirsk Museum, p153; Alistair Tosh, p47; Wakefield Historical Publications, p29; Whitbread (East Pennines) Ltd, p217; George Williamson, xviii; William Younger (Yorkshire) Ltd, p12, 13, 38, 121, 125, 131.

All other photographs are by Barrie Pepper.

ACKNOWLEDGEMENTS

I have picked many peoples' brains in preparing this book, and I have plundered many books and guides in search of good stories. I must thank the various branches of CAMRA for allowing me free access to their local real ale guides, particularly *North Yorkshire Ale,* without which it would not have been possible. Thanks to the many members of CAMRA, landlords, brewery staff and librarians who I have pestered to check facts and get it right. In particular, let me thank the following. Anne Heap, Joan Hewitt, Bill Park, Colin Waite and Michael Wayte. They know why. Posthumous thanks also to Alfred J Brown whose marvellous books on Yorkshire have reintroduced me to the county of my birth.

FOREWORD

Barrie Pepper has written a book which is very much like a pint of good ale. It has been lovingly brewed by a master of his subject. A splendidly anecdotal writing style provides a tempting head. Facts in plenty, sparklingly arrayed, form the body.

It is about Yorkshire inns and Yorkshire beer and Yorkshire brewers. The author is a Yorkshireman recognised as the county's leading writer on the pleasant pastime of beer drinking. He is also steeped in Yorkshire lore, and committed to Yorkshire traditions, including the preservation of the county's ancient Ridings. It is no surprise, then, that this book is more, far more, than a White Rose pub crawl. It is also about the county's history and its people, its industries and its great cities.

In Barrie Pepper, Yorkshire's pubs have found a true champion. He relates them firmly to their communities, and shows that despite the tendency towards uniformity encouraged by the breweries they often developed individual characteristics as pronounced as those of the people they served.

Readers will find him the most entertaining and knowledgeable of companions as he ranges the Ridings. It is a convivial journey indeed, a splendid way of imbibing facets of Yorkshire history. Many great characters crowd into the narrative, men and women with whom it would be a joy to take a drink.

Some were famous, like J B Priestley who wrote memorably of one inn as a 'haunt of rare souls'. Others are anonymous, like the labourer commemorated at the sign of the Blue Pig. He once scrubbed pigs with whitewash to which he had added some of his mother's dolly blue. There are also tall tales to swallow, of such things as ghosts and secret passages.

It is, then, a book to savour. Many will drain it to the last chapter and then wish for more. That, of course, is yet another characteristic of a pint of good ale.

Malcolm Barker

INTRODUCTION

This is not intended to be a guidebook, nor is it an academic tome. It reaches somewhere between the two, for there are pubs mentioned here that have long since gone and to which a visit would be fruitless, and there are tales told that the serious researcher would shy away from. But it does, I hope, point you to some interesting pubs that a visit will repay, though I make no apologies for the quality of ale you may find there. It did take an enormous amount of research, which my friends seemed to think was spent in pleasant tap rooms drinking excellent ale, when most of it was done in dusty libraries the length of the county.

I make no apologies, either, for widening the scope of this book to the real county of Yorkshire. I am firmly committed to the return of the Ridings and, in any case, even the most ardent local government reformer cannot but allow me to use the original boundaries when I am writing mainly about a period that fits within them.

It is impossible to say how many inns, pubs, taverns, dramshops, hotels and the like there have been in Yorkshire over the centuries, but a top-of-the-head guess would put it at around 20,000. It gives you some idea of the magnitude of the task of putting together such a book. I know I will have got it wrong and I know some people will take pleasure in pointing out my errors. I know I will have missed out some of the best tales and I know I will offend the regulars of a much loved, often a much missed, pub. I apologise in advance. I am anxious to know where I went wrong, what I missed out and what, hopefully, I can do to make it better next time. Ancient pubs can be found at once but good tales, as they say, take a little longer.

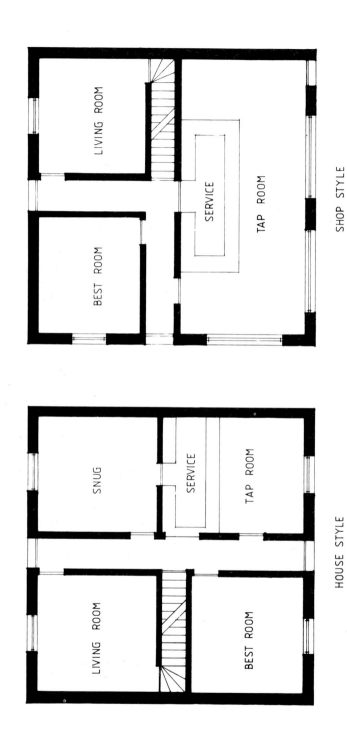

HOUSE STYLE

SHOP STYLE

The layout of pubs common to Yorkshire.

THE OLD INNS AND PUBS OF YORKSHIRE

'From hence we entered the great county of York, uncertain still which way to begin to take a full view of it, for 'tis a county of a very great extent.'

Daniel Defoe

Yorkshire can make no claims to have given birth to either beer or the public house. If to anyone, the credit should go to the Egyptians for one and the Romans for the other. But beer has been brewed here for at least 2,000 years and the county does possess both the oldest pub in England — the Bingley Arms at Bardsey — and the highest — the Tan Hill Inn on the Durham borders; and the pub, which is essentially an English institution, comes into its own in Yorkshire. That is, of course, the real Yorkshire of the three Ridings and the City of York.

The inn can properly be regarded as a rural institution, with the tavern and beerhouse as its urban relatives. The public house or pub, however, is a useful collective term. Yorkshire has a wide selection of all types of pubs: the gin palaces of the great cities as well as the downtown street corner locals, whilst the Dales have their village inns with post and coach houses on the main highways.

Yorkshire also has its own unique style of pub. It is more properly a West Riding genre — the 'house' style with its central corridor as a main drinking area and various rooms leading off. Good examples of this are the Gardeners Arms in Hunslet and the White Lion in Sheffield. Another style often found in Yorkshire is that of the 'shop' where a counter parallel to the front of the pub acts as the main bar, as in the Albion in Armley and the Mason Arms in Doncaster.

There must have been pubs in Yorkshire since the first century, and the Romans were known to have built *tabernae* (taverns) and *diversoriae* which developed into ale-houses. But the real history of the public house in the county starts 1,000 years later. The Bingley Arms at Bardsey to the east of Leeds is recognised in the *Guinness Book of Records* as the country's oldest inn, dating from the tenth century. It became a stopping off place between religious houses in Leeds and York, a similar function to that of the Cross Keys in Malton which, in the twelfth century, was a rest house for pilgrims. The Pack Horse in Leeds, of which little of the original remains these days, was a hostel for the Knights Templars in medieval days.

There are many rural inns of great age in the county, although few remain in the style they were built. They are like the 'original' village stocks, where the stone has been replaced twice and the wood four times. But such establishments as the Bridge at Ripponden and the Hark to Bounty at Slaidburn can count back to the thirteenth century, and the Ship Inn at Saltburn to the fifteenth.

The basic purpose of a public house is to provide refreshment for its customers, although until the later nineteenth century the service was generally of an appallingly low standard. Some improvements came about in Elizabethan times after a royal complaint about the standard of the nation's inns. (The Virgin Queen was a great traveller and the claim that 'Queen Elizabeth slept here' is no cliché.) One of the consequences was the building of a number of 'new' inns, some of which took that name; there are several in Yorkshire which have their origins in the late sixteenth and early seventeenth centuries. There are also New Taverns at Aislaby, Middleton near Pickering, Scarborough and Stokesley and, at North Newbold in the East Riding, there is a Gnu Inn!

During the eighteenth century the urban inns were often used for many other purposes, providing the focal point of a community. The magistrates often held court in them and the turnpike commissioners met there. They were stores and primitive shops, and often the innkeeper doubled up in other trades: the blacksmith, the cobbler, and the carpenter. From their trades the pub's name often followed: the Gardeners Arms in Hunslet, the Blacksmiths Arms at Swinton near Malton and the Cobblers at Pontefract. But surely the most unusual purpose to which an inn was put was at the Humber Tavern at Paull near Hull which, for a short period in 1836, acted as a lighthouse!

Some of these secondary businesses continue: the George at Wath near Pateley Bridge is also a sub-post office, the Old Bay Horse at Mickletown in the West Riding acts as a library, others sell seasonal fruits and vegetables, and the Newton in Sprotbrough near Doncaster is the venue for mass every Sunday morning in the absence of a Roman Catholic church in the village.

Economic and social factors affected the development of the inns, alehouses and taverns of Yorkshire through the ages, but nothing more drastically than transport. The county's geographic position midway between London and Edinburgh and the importance of the Great North Road were significant. As travel became an essential part of everyday life, then places of refreshment became essential too. Travellers needed sustenance and shelter — not just for themselves but for the horses that carried them. The pack horse and the lumbering wagons were replaced by speedy coaches, and more and more inns were built with facilities to meet these needs. Road improvements were made, and turnpikes or toll roads were built in the ever-increasing quest for speed. Competition was fierce and the inns were there to take advantage and meet the consequent need.

Yorkshire's first turnpike — between Doncaster and Saltersbrook which linked with a road from Manchester over Woodhead — was built in 1740. There were also roads from Doncaster to Borough-bridge, York, Wakefield and to the south. Doncaster was an important coaching centre and market town, and the number of pubs there reflected this. All along the Great North Road, the inns were strung out to cope with the many coaches and post horses that passed each day. The traffic also moved across the county and within the rapidly growing urban areas.

In 1753 the toll gate on the Harrogate turnpike at Harewood Bridge was attacked by a mob rebelling against the toll charges. The army was called in, three men were arrested and were taken to the Old Kings Arms in Leeds where the magistrates sat. There were ugly scenes, the Riot Act was read, soldiers fired on the mob and at least eight rioters died. But despite this and other disturbances, the number of turnpike roads continued to grow and with them were built the

The name and location of the Navigation at Calder Grove show its origins as a hostelry for barge crews.

inns needed to serve them. An Act of Parliament was necessary to authorise the construction of a turnpike, and the last major one was passed in 1832 for the road between Doncaster and Selby, following roughly the present A19.

Meanwhile, the waterway system was developing rapidly. Whilst the rest of Britain has canals, Yorkshire has navigations, that unique combination of canals and rivers which provide for commercial and pleasure traffic even to this day. Public houses were needed to serve the hard-worked crews of barges and keels that plied between collieries and ironworks and out to the Humber at Goole and Hull, and fortunately many of these canal and riverside inns remain with significant reminders in their names. The Navigation at Calder Grove and a similarly named one at Mirfield, the Ferry Boat at Mexborough, the Colliers at Elland and the Wharf at Sowerby Bridge are all good examples; and the Leeds and Liverpool Canal, although not completed until 1816, had its birth pangs in 1766 at the Sun Inn in Bradford, where a public meeting to launch the scheme was held.

Soon the days of the turnpikes were numbered, with the biggest and most enduring threat to the roads and their inns being the railways. Yorkshire's place in railway history is well-chronicled, but it is significant that it was in one of the county's public houses that a meeting took place which was not only to change the economic and industrial life of the nation but to direct its drinking habits over the next century. In 1820 the George and Dragon in Yarm High Street saw the inaugural meeting of the promoters of the Stockton and Darlington Railway — the first public railway in the world. A vast network of railways soon sprang up, and within the next fifty years fortunes were made and lost. The Leeds and Selby line opened in 1834 and five years later there was a link to York. By 1850 what became known as the East Coast main line had reached Doncaster and was soon built through to York, the North-East and Scotland.

The effect on the county's inns and pubs was twofold: coaching was dying and whilst roads were still essential the requirement for so many inns became less so, and a new breed of licensed house was being built — the railway hotel. They could be as modest as the L & Y R Hotel

6

The railways brought a new type of pub — the railway hotel. A modest
example was the L & Y R Hotel in Knottingley.

in Knottingley, the Midland in Skipton and the Queen in Todmorden, or large and impressive like Bradford's Victoria, the Station
(now the Royal Station) in York and the Zetland at Saltburn.
Coaching inns like the Old Angel in Doncaster vanished in this
period, along with the George Inn and Etteridges Hotel in York, the
Rose and Crown in Easingwold and the Greyhound at Ferrybridge.

The middle of the nineteenth century saw other changes, both
legislative and social, which affected the numbers and types of public
houses in the county. The evils of gin drinking — the so-called
'mother's ruin' — had prompted the government to act. Wellington's
administration brought in the Beerhouse Act of 1830, which aimed to
reduce spirit drinking by making beer more accessible. Under the act,

any person of good character could purchase a licence for two guineas and set up a beerhouse, and the duty on beer was halved. The number of licensed premises in England and Wales doubled in ten years with a remarkable 25,000 licences being taken out within three months of the act becoming law. In Leeds the number increased from 270 to 545 by 1837.

Another effect of the act was to increase the dominance of the common brewer, people who brewed to sell to other outlets rather than for themselves. There was already a firm base in Yorkshire, with large breweries at Sheffield, Halifax, Huddersfield, Leeds and Tadcaster, yet more than half of the ale brewed in the county was produced by the owners of pubs themselves. But many of the new beerhouses were simple places with no facilities to brew, so new breweries were built and others rapidly increased their production. The Gilmour Brewery in Sheffield opened in 1831, to be followed in 1834 by Thomas Walker at Kirkstall and John J Hunt in York, and later in the decade came the Fountain Brewery in Bradford. By the turn of the century, home brewing accounted for less than fifteen per cent of production.

Whilst the name of the Duke of Wellington is the one that has lasted into the history books as the author of the Beerhouse Act, it was King William IV who took the credit in a popular song of the day:

'Come one and all, both great and small,
With voices loud and clear,
And let us sing ''Bless Billy the King'',
Who bated the tax upon beer.'

The rise in the popularity of horse racing and the allied gambling had a small but significant effect on the development of the county's inns and pubs. Yorkshire has more than thirty pubs named after racehorses — probably more than any other county — and considerably more with names associated with the sport. Many of them were built in the the nineteenth century following the success of a horse in a classic race — and often a massive winning bet. The Little Wonder at Harrogate is named after a fifty to one Derby winner; the Altisidora at Bishop Burton after a St Leger winner; and one of the most

PUBS NAMED AFTER
RACE HORSES
(In most cases a reference will
be found in the text)

YORK
PAREFOOT ■
BAY MALTON ■
BEESWING
BRIGADIER GERARD ■
ECLIPSE
FLYING DUTCHMAN
FROGHALL
OLD EPOR
TAM O' SHANTER ■

RACECOURSE
CLASSIC WINNER ■
GRAND NATIONAL WINNER ▲

* RACECOURSE
■ CLASSIC WINNER
▲ GRAND NATIONAL WINNER

SHEFFIELD
BEESWING ■
CREMORNE
COSSACK
WELL RUN DIMPLE
WHY NOT ▲

REDCAR *

▲ TEAL

VOLTIGEUR ○
BEESWING ○
REVELLERS ○
NON PLUS ○
OCTAVIAN ○

○ MOORCOCK
○ POVERINA

QUEEN OF TRUMPS

GREY DESIRE ○
○ ALICE HAWTHORNE

* THIRSK

* YORK
MARCIA ○
CHARLES XII ○
○ ALICE HAWTHORNE

DON JUAN ■ ○ ALTISIDORA

NANCY ○

* BEVERLEY

○ MARE PHOENIX

RIPON *

FLYING DUTCHMAN ○
LITTLE WONDER ○

WETHERBY *

○ HIGHFLYER
○ ARKLE

GREAT NORTH ROAD

PONTEFRACT *

▲ RED RUM
FLYING DUTCHMAN ■
DON JUAN

DONCASTER *

RIDGEWOOD ○
ROCKINGHAM *
○ FLYING CHILDERS

● SHEFFIELD

The start of the temperance movement in the shadow of a brewery!

successful horses of all time, the Alice Hawthorn, the outright winner of fifty-one races, has two houses to remember it by, at Weldrake and Nun Monkton. The latest in this long series is the Red Rum at Grimethorpe, commemorating its three wins in the Grand National. The horse itself performed the opening ceremony with great style and dignity.

The number of public houses in Yorkshire peaked around 1875 at more than 10,000. But the increased use of railways, better roads, and legislation which brought the issue of licences once more under the control of the bench of magistrates, all pointed to a significant drop in their number. By the turn of the century nearly 1,000 had lost their licences.

There was a compensating factor in the genesis of the working men's clubs movement. At first many of these were teetotal establishments, reflecting the rise of the temperance movement in the area. (The Band of Hope was formed in 1847 in the shadow of Tetley's brewery at Leeds!) Later the clubs provided the artisan with companionship, social interests and cheap beer.

Beer retained a respectable image despite the efforts of the temperance movement, and was still regarded by many as the 'safe' alternative to spirits. Hogarth's cartoons of Gin Lane, with its decrepit and haggard spirit 'topers', and Beer Street, showing the healthy and cheerful ale 'suppers', epitomised this. There was a boost in the 1860's with the building of massive reservoirs in the lower Dales to supply the West Riding towns with water. Up to then, Leeds water had been pumped straight from the River Aire, which also served as the main sewer. (There were similar conditions elsewhere.) The new 'water bright' had a marked effect on the quality of beer, although many breweries took water from their own wells.

The turn of the last century was significant. The cities of Sheffield, Bradford and Leeds were growing rapidly, the motor car was in its naissance and the magistrates were demanding better standards from the owners of public houses. It was also a peak period for drunkenness: during 1900 more than 22,000 convictions were registered in the county. Compensation could also now be paid to the pub owners if the magistrates considered their establishments were inadequate in their facilities, or that there were too many pubs in an area. Thousands closed and in many cases were demolished. Coupling these factors with the increased powers given to local authorities led to improved standards for pubs, particularly in the cities.

It was also the period of the high Victorian and Edwardian splendour of the provincial gin palaces of Leeds, Hull and Sheffield — built to meet the needs of the middle classes — and the spa hotels of Scarborough, Ilkley and Harrogate. It also marked a period of rebuilding for many street corner pubs to save them from the clutches of the justices. Similar commercial factors were to determine the style and spread of the pub in Yorkshire over the next half century.

At this time the common brewers were taking a tighter grip by investing more and more in their own pubs — the tied houses. Remarkably it was 1890 before Tetleys bought their first pub, the Duke William, a bargee's house almost within the brewery. Other breweries had small estates but now the race was on. The Melbourne Brewery in Leeds was the most aggressive acquisitor, employing a spy system to ascertain the trade of every outlet in Leeds and Bradford. There were detailed records:

'Accommodation Inn, Upper Accommodation Road, Leeds. Joseph Pickersgill, Albion brewery. P, who was in possession for 5 years under Findlays and later Albion says he did 9 to 11 hogsheads of Common ale, 1 h/hd of Old and 1 h/hd Bitter per week. 20% discount and 80% long pull. 20 dozen bottles per week. Known locally as ''The Granny''. Owned by Miss Nicholson of Roundhay Road.'

Brewery estates grew larger and more valuable, and competition was rife. The rather curious 'long pull' was one of the weapons the landlords in the towns and cities used to keep their pubs full. After receiving the first pint, the customer would drink about three-quarters of it and offer back the glass. The landlord would fill it up but charge only for half a pint. The practice was outlawed and eventually made illegal.

The Great War brought other changes in the shape of the Defence of the Realm Act, with its severe restrictions on licensing hours. Up to the middle of the nineteenth century there had been no limitations, and since then pubs were only required to close during the night hours. In slightly amended shape the much hated DORA remained in force until 1988 when all-day opening was once more allowed.

The twenties and thirties saw new styles of pub architecture intro-duced and, thankfully, another wave of improvements in public houses. Takeovers of small breweries left the larger regional companies with an assortment of houses in varying degrees of condition. Amongst the new pubs were some large freestanding roadhouses with massive car parks (more popular in the Home Counties than in Yorkshire) built on the county's main roads, such as Punchs Hotel on the Great North Road near Doncaster and the Buckles on the dual carriageway between Tadcaster and York. Other reminders of the period are the big pubs built to service large housing estates, like the Middleton Arms in South Leeds, the Wellington at Athersley in Barnsley and the Barrowcliffe in Scarborough.

The pubs of the forties and fifties are an austere lot, and few breweries in the county got their act together to create originality and style. Architects had more on their minds in solving the massive housing problems and rebuilding the commercial and industrial

An example of the changes in pub styles during the 1930's:

the Bee Hive Hotel in Wakefield before and after substantial alterations.

structure of the nation. Certainly no style has developed, and the only positive contribution to the pub's evolution has been the move by some brewers to renovate some of their older houses in a sensitive fashion in an effort to restore them to their former grandeur. Tetleys introduced their Heritage Inns scheme and, of the twenty or so completed so far, the Black Horse in Whitby, the Bath in Sheffield, the Garden Gate in Hunslet and the Spotted Cow in Malton are good examples.

All the county's brewers have carried out improvements and alterations to their pubs with varying degrees of success. In many cases the alterations have been to detriment of their customers, damaging to aesthetics and often to the brewers' own cost. But this contemporary discussion is one beyond the scope of this book. A thousand years of the public house in Yorkshire is topic enough.

THE GREAT NORTH ROAD
THROUGH DONCASTER

'Doncaster, a place noted for its races, locomotives, markets and butterscotch...'
Douglas Bolton

Entering Yorkshire from the south by the Great North Road brings you to Bawtry, where in medieval days the Sheriff of Nottingham would greet the king with a purse of gold. It was an important staging post on the Great North Road for the coaching and posting trade, and in the late eighteenth century there was little else there except a Saturday market and the occasional horse fair.

The town's first coaching inn was the Swan. It took up much of the village, with its houses for the postboys and stabling, as well as the inn itself. Later, about 1800, the Crown took over the posting business and the accolade of the 'top inn'. There is a claim that it got its name after the sheriff procured it for the king after the landlord had been arrested for harbouring outlaws, including the notorious gang of Robin Hood. It was also a haven for highwaymen, whose accomplices would ply rich visitors with drink and then ambush them as they went on their way. Dick Turpin is said to have frequented the place, and once rode Black Bess up the front steps. The older parts are reputed to be haunted by a well-dressed elderly lady — she may even be the ubiquitous 'grey lady' that will appear so often in this book.

Doncaster's inns knew the famed and the famous, from James I who stayed at the Old Angel in Frenchgate in 1603, to the many jockeys and other racing personalities who have attended race meetings here. Several authors have put to paper their views on this town: Daniel Defoe found curiosity in the fact that one innkeeper should also be its mayor; and Arnold Bennett commented on the rougher side of racing.

Racing has been a major influence in the history of Doncaster's inns and pubs, but coaching was the predominant one. The Old Angel not

only attracted King James — he was followed by the Duke of York and the Prince of Wales in 1778, and the prince returned again in 1795. References can be found to the inn as far back as 1458, when it was probably called the Bear. When Richard Whitaker was its landlord in 1700, the corporation voted him £12 to provide brisket and sack for the judges and aldermen at each assize. Whitaker himself became mayor in 1728, an event which caused Defoe to write:
'...landlord at the post house was Mayor, postmaster, kept a pack of hounds, was company for the best gentlemen in the town...and lived as great as any gentlemen ordinarily did.'

Richard Whitaker received £6 from the town council during his year of office to provide music for ceremonials, which caused a local wag to pen the following:

> 'The Doncaster Mayor sits in his chair,
> His mills they merrily go,
> His nose doth shine with drinking wine,
> And the gout is in his great toe.'

Whitaker's son James took over the licence of the Old Angel from his father and, in 1760, also became mayor of the town. Another visitor was the Reverend William MacRichie, an intrepid traveller who recorded his visit there in the summer of 1795:

'Thursday 13th August...Night comes on as we approach to the boundary of Yorkshire...converse about robbers: no guard attends us: all of us unarmed. Arrive at Doncaster at eleven pm, thank God, without any untoward accident having befallen us. Sup, ten gentlemen together. At three quarters past eleven, the coach sets forward with my fellow-travellers, whom I recommend to the protection of Heaven, and rest here all night in a good comfortable inn. Friday 14th August. Doncaster. Slept soundly for eight hours at the Angel Inn, one of the best inns in England.'

Celia Fiennes, one of the first women to travel round the country and document her journeys, said she was well entertained at the Angel but not so in Mansfield and Buxton. The Old Angel was demolished in 1846 and the following year the Guildhall was built on the site.

In 1810 another Angel had appeared in the town. Known as the

Richard (Dickey) Wood, Doncaster's principal coach proprietor.

New Angel, it was later called the Angel and Royal after Queen Victoria and Prince Albert visited there in 1851. The Royal Mail coaches left here for London and the landlord who saw the demise of the coaching trade, Thomas Pye, used to drive the Edinburgh mail himself between Doncaster and Stamford. It was demolished in 1964 to make way for a shopping centre.

There were many other coaching inns in the town, including the Reindeer, where the redoubtable Dickey Wood stabled 200 horses and had John Frederick Herring, who later made a fortune as a painter of animals and particularly racehorses, as his coachman and coachpainter. Herring also painted many of the town's inn signs.

Dickey Wood was the principal coach proprietor in the town and had his offices at the Reindeer, which was built in 1780 and substantially altered in 1837. It was here that Arnold Bennett recorded in 1897 a conversation he had about the rough elements in racing. He wrote that the landlord carried a loaded revolver with him at all times and had told him:

'This place at racetimes is simply hell. We have two policemen continually at the foot of the steps and at any moment eight more can be summoned in fifteen seconds.'

The Reindeer was pulled down in 1960.

The Red Lion in the market place was built in 1742 and was the location of a famous meeting that is well-established in the history of horse racing. A breakfast was held there in 1778 to give a title to a successful but yet unnamed race for three year olds that had been held for the past two years. Present were the Marquis of Rockingham and his agent, Colonel Anthony Saint Leger, together

The Red Lion, birthplace of the St Leger.

with the Squire of Cantley. The squire suggested the Rockingham Stakes, as the marquis had put up the prize money, but the peer insisted on it taking the name of his servant who had thought up the idea of such a race. The St Leger is the oldest and longest of the five Classic races run in the flat season. Some records show the Salutation as being the birthplace of the race, but it is probably here that the original one was conceived. There is a St Leger Tavern in Silver Street which has existed since 1822, which was formerly called the Three Jolly Blacksmiths.

The Horse and Jockey in St Sepulchre Gate — once called the Horse and Groom — was built in 1815. The Turf Tavern in St James Street, built in 1826, had stables added to it for the purpose of breeding racehorses in 1829. Lord George Bentinct brought his stud here in 1833 where it stayed until 1846 when he severed his connections with racing. It was to the Turf Tavern that the first ever horsebox carried Elis, the 1836 St Leger winner, from Goodwood. It carried two horses, had a padded floor and sides and was drawn by six post horses. The Ridgewood at Edenthorpe is named after a one hundred to seven winner of the St Leger, whilst the Beechers Brook at Cantley is named after a fence on the Grand National course at Aintree.

Sprotborough has a clutch of interesting pubs. Walter Scott is said to have written *Ivanhoe* at the Ferry Boat Inn, now part of a farm, although there is a large village inn with its own cricket pitch called the Ivanhoe. The Boat, none too tastefully modernised these days, was once a farm alehouse; and the Newton is used every Sunday to celebrate mass in the absence of a Roman Catholic church for the area.

Ghosts and legends abound in the area's pubs. The 200 year old Crown at Askern has a 'locked in' ghost. An unused room on the second floor not only had bars to the windows but several locks and bolts on the outside. The daughter of a former landlord slept there once and said she 'sensed a presence', claiming the curtains opened on their own. Other people said that from the next door bathroom they heard noises from the room when no-one was in there.

At Campsall there is a claim that the Old Bells is 800 years old, but the age of its 'grey lady' ghost is unknown. It is also said to have a secret passage to the nearby church. Here another piece of the Robin Hood jigsaw can be found, for it is where he was supposed to have been married. There is other evidence that he frequented the area: at Robin Hoods Well on the Great North Road there were two inns, the Robin Hood and the New Inn, to cope with the thirty coaches and more a day that passed through as well as with other traffic.

The Robin Hood and Little John at Hatfield Woodhouse is another reminder of the outlaw. At Hatfield, the Bay Horse dates back to the seventeenth century, and the Green Tree to the sixteenth. The latter was an alehouse that later took on some posting business. It is said that on the same night as the Battle of Marston Moor in 1644 when Cromwell routed the Royalist troops, a group of retreating Cavaliers found a Roundhead staying at the Green Tree and hung him from a beam in his room. Needless to say he has haunted the place ever since!

There were several coaching houses in Thorne, including the White Hart, dating from 1737, where post coaches from Doncaster and Sheffield would call on their way to Hull; and the Old John Bull, which was a transfer point for steam packets to Hull, presumably sailing along the 'Dutch River' and then the Humber.

Ferrybridge was a vital coach junction for the routes north to Edinburgh through Tadcaster and York, to Aberford and over Stainmore to Carlisle, and to Leeds by way of Peckfield Bar. In its heyday the Angel was the most important house, kept by Doctor George Alderson, general practicioner, coach proprietor and Rector of Birkin. It was claimed as 'the best known coaching house on the Great North Road'. Other houses included the Greyhound, which was the 'tap' for post boys and horsemen. The Golden Lion remains an impressive inn, with its location on the River Aire able to provide interchanges between coaches and river boats to Hull. It also horsed coaches, using the Swan across the bridge in Brotherton. But the Fox, these days a roadhouse, and the Red Bear at Sherburn-in-Elmet, were then basic places used by the Scottish drovers heading south with their cattle.

The Fox at Brotherton, formerly used by the Scottish drovers on their way south.

A claim to be the oldest house on the Great North Road is made for the Blue Bell at Wentbridge. There was an old sign kept in the house of the 'Blue Bell on Wentbridge Hill' dated 1633, though it is also said that it is older and more than 400 years ago it lost its licence for harbouring poachers and footpads. The Crown at Monk Fryston is an old stone structure with existing outbuildings, and the now closed Chequers has the remains of the tiny brewery of Thomas Berry behind it. The quaintly named Queen O' Towd Thatch at South Milford dates from 1720 and was thatched until the beginning of this century — the name simply meaning a pub called the Queen with an old thatched roof.

Behind Selby's magnificent abbey can be found the Crown. Tales of a ghost started when a barman claimed to see the ubiquitous 'grey lady', and noises were heard in an empty next door building. But one Christmas Day the landlord, landlady and several customers saw an old picture of the pub fly off the wall across the bar and smash on the floor. It is known that a former landlord murdered his wife in the bar after a heavy drinking session during the Christmas period, and speculation has it that the 'grey lady' is the murdered woman.

The Londesborough Arms is an eighteenth century hotel and was Selby's top coaching inn, vying with the Black-a-Moor Head for that privilege. The Griffin, in splendid art nouveau style, was built by Bentleys of Woodlesford in 1900 on the site of an old brewery, and the New Inn in Gowthorpe, a one time town house, is a Tetley Heritage Inn that bears traces of its former owners, Middlebrough of Selby. It retains some excellent stained glass, panelling and glazed screens. To the front is a small panelled tap room with a serving hatch that is known as the 'Vatican'.

For many years Barkston Ash gave its name to a parliamentary constituency, although it was probably the smallest hamlet within it. Here the Ash Tree Inn is reputed to be at the dead centre of Yorkshire's three Ridings. At nearby Saxton can be found the Greyhound, which must make the claim to be one of the best examples of an unspoilt village pub in Yorkshire. Nothing seems to have changed since around the turn of the century. The barrels are racked behind the bar, the floors are stone flagged, the roof is thatched, and pub games like 'devil amongst the tailors' are played in the tap room. The Battle of Towton, possibly the bloodiest in the War of the Roses, was fought nearby and in the adjacent churchyard can be found the tombstone of Lord Dacre, one of the many Lancastrian nobles who died in the battle.

Cawood has one pub of great antiquity, with its origins in the sixteenth century, although the present building dates from only 1872. The Ferry Inn — formerly the Commercial and before that the Ferryboat — can be found next to the bridge on the riverbank, and in times past it was the ferry house. But Cawood is best known in a drinking sense by the Great Feast of 1465 to celebrate the elevation of Archbishop George Neville to the See of York. In addition to the 100 oxen, 500 deer and 1,000 sheep that were eaten, 300 tuns of ale went down the throats of the guests — that means 600,000 pints!

Tadcaster is better known by its breweries than its pubs. The quality of its well water has made it known locally as 'the Burton of the North' and, even today when small and medium-sized breweries bite the dust with sickening regularity, three in Tadcaster — all a century or more old — appear to be doing thriving business.

Tadcaster was an important coaching town on the Great North Road run from London to York and the North, and on the west-east routes from Leeds and Lancashire. At its height more than fifty coaches a day passed through there. The White Swan in Bridge Street is the only remaining coaching inn, although the present Angel and White Horse has its origins in two former inns.

The Angel was originally called the Red Hart. It was built in the early eighteenth century and stands where the present Angel and White Horse now is. Along with many other similar licensed houses that depended on the coaching and post trade, it closed in 1855 as the railways developed their extensive networks. A similar fate had applied to the White Horse next door in 1841. Matthew Kidd was the licensee of the Angel; he had been born there and followed his father into the job. Lord Londesborough bought the White Horse to accomodate his racing guests and to make it the top hotel in Tadcaster. He negotiated for the licence of the Angel with Kidd, who agreed to sell if he could become the landlord. He did so and stayed there for ten years. The Angel eventually became shops, and the Londesborough Hotel was opened. It stayed that way until 1976. The new pub, which acts as a flagship for Samuel Smith's brewery, opened two years later.

The White Swan remains, although it is much altered. A former landlord, Joseph Middleton, lived there through five reigns — from George III to Edward VII. The oldest coaching inn was probably the Rose and Crown on the east side of the bridge (which splits the town and was once the boundary between the West Riding and the Ainsty of York). It was worked in conjunction with the Post Office, where the postmaster John Hartley ran what was described 'as important a coaching establishment as any of the inns'. Across the bridge was the

Golden Lion — traces of which can still be seen — which was used by the heavy coaches that carried baggage and boxes of fish; their cumbersome progress lead to the term 'slow coach'.

The Howden Arms in the high street was not a coaching inn and remains now as it was when built in 1763, essentially a locals' house. (The early nineteenth century Falcon Inn is a similar sort of pub.) There was an Old Falcon Inn in Kirkgate in the town's oldest building, now the Ark Museum, which has many artefacts from the brewing industry and memories of the town's pubs. Also in Kirkgate, where a shop now stands, was the Bull and Dog, which changed its name to the Railway Hotel in 1837 as the new method of transport drew nearer. It was the proud boast that a carriage from here met every train at Bolton Percy Station before the line reached Tadcaster. Ironically its landlord, Godfrey Braim, was killed in a rail accident at Church Fenton Station in 1856 and his tombstone is in Tadcaster churchyard.

Stutton stands apart from Tadcaster, with the Hare and Hounds as its focal point. It probably has seventeenth century origins and claims as a resident one of the county's more exotic ghosts. It is a prince in black armour and dates from a battle long ago during which the building was used as a hospital.

On the western side of the road in the historic and delightful village of Ledsham is the Chequers, a classic rambling country pub which dates from the seventeenth century. It has a licence that prohibits drinking on Sunday — one of only two in Yorkshire. The Chequers is on land owned by the Lady Elizabeth Hastings Estate Charities, which imposed its unique licensing restriction around the turn of the century after trouble with some rowdy drinkers. Lady Betty, as she was known, lived at nearby Ledston Hall in the eighteenth century. She was a formidable lady, a pillar of the church who endowed an orphanage and, according to Nicholas Pevsner, 'was praised universally for her intellect and virtue'. In nearby Ledston the White Horse is a former farmhouse dating from the early eighteenth century, where Dick Turpin is said to have evaded his pursuers by hiding in a chimney breast.

At Aberford, an attractive village which straddles the old Great North Road, is the impressive Swan Hotel. It dates from the sixteenth century and was a regular halt for coaches on the run between London and Edinburgh during the eighteenth and nineteenth centuries. (The post house where the Royal Mail coaches changed their horses was opposite the Swan.) Through the arch of the pub are stables marked with the sign 'J. Heaton — Licensed to Let Post Horses' and under the arch is the old coaching bell which warned passengers of the imminent departure of their transport.

On the village green is the Arabian Horse, built in 1770 and first known as the Bay Horse. The change came about around 1850 when a group of the first Arabian racehorses in England were stranded in the village on their way to the training gallops at Middleham. It is the only licensed house in Britain with such a name. The pub still proudly displays two magnificent fireplaces, one of which is more than 200 years old and was only discovered in 1975. At the beginning of the nineteenth century there were nine pubs in Aberford — as befits

The uniquely-named Arabian Horse at Aberford.

In its heyday the Angel in Wetherby had stabling for 100 horses.

an important halt on the Great North Road — but now only three remain.

Wetherby's reputation as a overnight stopping point for most of the fast coaches on the road was enhanced because the town is just about halfway between London and Edinburgh. There are several inns here that can claim longevity, like the Swan and Talbot, which is more than 400 years old and was originally known just as the Talbot. The name is a combination of two of the oldest and best known pub signs (the talbot is an extinct breed of hunting dog). The Angel, more than 200 years old, has a fine sign showing a very fierce St Michael the Archangel holding a sword and shield. In the 1880's a set of murals of Bible scenes was discovered there under several layers of wallpaper. In its heyday as a coaching inn, the Angel had stabling for more than 100 horses.

The Angel and the Talbot were the most important of Wetherby's coaching inns, and following the 'great fire of Wetherby' in 1723, when around fifty properties were destroyed, both were insured with the Sun Fire Office for £1,000. With the arrival of the railways, the coach traffic suffered and many inns were forced to close. By 1848 the only coaches running through Wetherby were on the east-west routes between Leeds and York, but horse-drawn buses met trains at Wetherby Station and the two hotels continued to flourish, particularly during the period of race meetings.

WAKEFIELD — THE 'MERRIE CITY'

'...it was a common saying that there were three strange wants in Wakefield: a parson wanting pride, young men wanting wives, and ale-houses wanting customers.'

Oliver Goldsmith

Wakefield — the 'Merrie city' — possibly got the tag because of the number of pubs there, but the local branch of the Campaign for Real Ale find no reason to continue to justify it, particularly in the town centre, because of the number of insensitive refurbishments by the big brewers in recent years. Not all have had this treatment, but the gems that are left are few and far between.

Wakefield's most celebrated inn was the White Hart in Little Westgate. Henry Clarkson in his *Memories of Merry Wakefield* referred to it as the 'principal inn and posting house of the town'. It was large with a pebble-dashed front, and a wide archway led to the yard in which there were stables to one side and the town's assembly rooms to the other, where fashionable gatherings were held. The rooms were demolished in 1820 and the pub fifteen years later. The Strafford Arms was originally built in the fifteenth century, rebuilt in the eighteenth and again a few years ago. It was an important hostelry and a contemporary record understated it as 'where coaches stopped'.

The Original Alfred Moodies in Bread Street is an historic pub, though thoroughly spoiled by successive changes. It was once a wine and spirit merchant's shop. The splendid facade of the Elephant and Castle in Westgate is matched by the excellent windows of the Swan with Two Necks across the road. Both are Victorian, as is the Redoubt in Horbury Road which has been variously named the Drovers Inn and the Spotted Cow. It takes its present name from a Royal Navy warship, although there have been claims that it is connected with the Crimean War. Tetleys named it a Heritage Inn and the present layout of many rooms and some fine glasswork fully justify this.

Parts of the Red Lion in Ossett are said to be 400 years old, and it

The Strafford Arms was originally built in the fifteenth century.

is within these parts that the resident ghost is seen. Despite the town's inland location, it is haunted by a sailor wearing a wide hat, sea boots and a cloak, who walks with a limp. The story has it that he hung himself from a beam in the pub. The Red Lion is one of a number of relatively unspoilt pubs in the town. The Royal Oak in Gawthorpe is the starting point each year for one of Yorkshire's many bizarre sporting events — the World Coal Carrying Championship. Men have to run 1,080 yards from the pub to the town maypole carrying a hundredweight sack of coal. For women the distance and weight are less.

There were six public houses and a number of unlicensed ale houses in Walton at one time, but only one, the New Inn, remains. The Cross Keys lost its licence in unusual circumstances. In the early days of the nineteenth century it was a well-run posting house, but later it was taken over by Jimmy Vickers, who had three lovely daughters. Their attractions brought many admirers to the inn, and of course they drank well of its other attractions.

THE INNS OF PONTEFRACT.

One day, **Robin Hood** and his merry men set off from the **New Inn** to visit their companions in the **Ancient Borough.** They held a **Nag's Head** awhile, until they heard the **Blue Bell** ringing in the **United Kingdom,** from which they boarded a **Mail Coach,** setting out on which they passed a place containing the dead bodies of many beasts, and saw a **Red Lion** and **Elephant** closely attended by a **Black Boy.** They next cleaved the **Turk's Head** and proceeded to oust the **Fox** from his lair. Then they rested themselves under the leaves of a **Royal Oak,** and beheld in the distance the celebrated **Leap of Nevison.** They then **Anchored** awhile with **Hope** of that name, to view in the background that product of civilization, the **Railway Hotel.** Marching back to the town, they proceeded to storm the **Old Castle** under the command of the immortal **Wellington.** Seeking fresh fields and pastures new, they beheld in their journey a **Woodman** in the act of felling a tree, and a **Dolphin** flapping his fins in the Fair; also a dead **White Swan** slain by a man named Hartley. Rolling past a **Golden Ball** they refreshed themselves with a little **Pine Apple,** then proceeded onwards. Leaving the **Rose** to its own **Crown** and the **Windmill** with its flowing sails and Magnet Ales, they dined with the **Corporation** at the **Arms,** in Salter Row. Resting awhile they proceeded on their journey, and passed a **Blackamoor** watching a **White Hart,** and still further the curious sight of that relic of pre-historic times a **Green Dragon,** and a **Gardener** with folded **Arms** watching a **Greyhound** competing with a **Golden Lion** for a **Queen's** Prize. Wandering aimlessly back, they found a **Malt Shovel,** leaning up close by side with a **Crown and Anchor.** Turning at this stage into a network of lanes, they beheld a **Currier** folding in his **Arms** a **Cross of Keys,** and a **Cartner's Arms,** held out in meek supplication to the Established Church, never to withhold its present intervention between him and his isolated neighbour the **Starkie's.**

The Inns of Pontefract by Michael Philbin.

Drunken scenes were commonplace, and the frequent disturbances led to complaints by neighbours. The justices took note and Jimmy's licence was withdrawn.

At Sandal, the Three Houses was originally built in the seventeenth century. It is where the highwayman John Nevison — 'Swift Nick' as Charles II called him — was arrested after his famous ride from London, which is often credited to Dick Turpin.

The Junction at Featherstone was built some time in the early nineteenth century, but was extended around 1890 when John Waller, 'farmer and threshing machine proprietor', was the landlord. He had an imposing tower brewery behind the pub, and his son was the brewer of 'Fine Home Brewed Ales'.

Inns and pubs often feature in the social history of a place, and so it is with Featherstone's Railway Hotel, once known as the Heywood Arms after Lord Heywood who lived at Aketon Hall. It was built in 1845 and it was here that the inquest was held on James Gibbs, one of the two men who died in the Featherstone 'Massacre' in 1893. There had been a demand by the coal owners to cut miners' wages, which was resisted by strikes. Lockouts followed and a picket was mounted to stop blacklegs moving coal from Aketon Hall Colliery. The police were occupied at Doncaster Races so the troops were called in from the barracks at Pontefract. The Riot Act was read, the troops opened fire and two men, including Gibbs, were killed.

Records of the Poll Tax of 1379 help to identify the number of publicans in a town, and it appears that Pontefract had four. What is more, while the standard tax was fourpence, for taverners it was sixpence and this included all people living in the premises. (One wonders if Wat Tyler's rebellion two years later was inspired by the licensed trade.)

Court records in the town show the appointment of two ale tasters in 1788, and then regularly until 1793. One of them was also the pindar, who looked after the pinfold where stray animals were impounded until released on payment of a fine. Where the pinfold stood in Gillygate was built the Turks Head, previously known as the Falcon and later the Red Bear.

Landlord, friend and neighbours outside the Starkies Arms.

The Starkies Arms, now part of the market hall, was built in the early nineteenth century and named after Nicholas Starkie, who was elected a Member of Parliament in 1832. On the 18th January 1830, William Robert Shepherd, the licensee, was convicted for 'suffering tippling in his house on the previous Christmas Day during the hours of divine service'. Ten years later, twelve licensees were convicted at the quarter sessions for permitting ale to be drunk during afternoon divine service. Starkies closed down between the wars, as did many others.

Long distance coaching continued in Pontefract until around 1850, with regular services to London, Glasgow, Sheffield and Leeds, and to Hull after changing to steam packets at Knottingley. The Royal Mail left the Star Inn in the market place each morning on its route from Glasgow to London, and in the other direction in the afternoon. The Star, which is known to have existed since 1634, was the venue for a famous cockfighting match arranged by the gentlemen of Pontefract and the gentlemen of Leeds in 1739. Thomas Fisher was the host and there were ten matches with stakes at five guineas each. The end of coaching brought the demise of this pub.

The Red Lion is an early eighteenth century inn and coaching house. It has a facade added in 1776 that was designed by Robert Adam when he was working at Nostell Priory. It was here in 1725 that the innkeepers of Pontefract organised the first horse races in Pontefract Park. The Malt Shovel has a vaulted stone cellar that dates from the fourteenth century. It was a coaching inn as late as 1878, running a twice-daily service from here to nearby Castleford — with extra services on Tuesdays and Saturdays. The splendid foursquare Flying Horse in Salter Row dates from the seventeenth century. The current name is modern, changing from the Corporation Arms in 1963. Another pub that changed its name at that time was the present Ancient Borough Arms, known previously as Brices Vaults since it was owned by the chemists, Brice and Butler, in 1860. It included a public bar known as the 'Long Bar', a ladies-only bar and an off licence fronting the market place.

Castleford can be said to be a rival of Pontefract in many ways, but not so in the historic value of its inns and pubs. In the town have been found Roman remains, including drinking vessels and what may have been malted barley, an indication that drinking took place there 2,000 years ago. What may be the oldest existing pub in the town is the Shoulder of Mutton on the Methley Road; it has a low ceiling and retains its traditional layout, and dates from the late eighteenth century. The Crimea Tavern also retains a good deal of style despite modernisation. It was a coaching inn and the arched gate into a yard remains. In Church Street the Horse and Jockey, a basic boozer, has a splendid set of 1907 handpumps. The railway's arrival meant the conversion of a large house opposite the station into the North Eastern Hotel. It advertised '...well matured wines of rare quality...' and '...cigars of best quality at moderate prices'.

At Whitwood is a most unusual pub, the Rising Sun. It started out life in 1905 as a colliery institute in a purpose-designed building by the

The Crimea in Castleford was a coaching inn, and its arched gateway remains.

The Rising Sun at Whitwood was formerly a miners' institute. Note the three storey tower.

architect C F A Voysey. It has some interesting shapes, including a three storey tower, and fits in with an adjoining row of cottages built by the same man. It is listed by the Department of the Environment as a building of architectural and historic interest and the blueprints are displayed inside.

There is a 'Hark to' inn at Normanton. This is the Hark to Mopsey with the derivation arising from a hound called Mopsey, possibly the pack leader, whose distinctive sound could be heard when he picked up the scent. It has an interesting exterior with the name picked out in stone above a castellated gable. Other 'Hark to' inns in Yorkshire include the Hark to Bounty at Slaidburn, the Hark to Rover at Kirkstall in Leeds and the Hark to Nudger at Dobcross on the old Lancashire border. The Normanton Hotel was built in 1840 with stone taken from a cutting for the laying of the Midland railway. The Flying Scotsman in Railway Terrace is the station pub although the former express did not run through Normanton, despite its one time importance as a railway junction. In nearby Altofts the Lee Brigg, a pleasant Victorian house, takes its name from Lee's Bridge which once spanned the local brook. As a notice on the front of the pub states: 'Both bridge and brook have since disappeared — the bridge into history, the brook underground'.

The village of South Kirkby has seen its public houses put to some unusual uses. The Rose and Crown, originating from the seventeenth century, was built near to the village church to provide refreshment for worshippers from nearby townships before starting the long walk home. It was rebuilt in 1960. The top floor of Old Crown, the only three storey building in South Kirkby, was the union headquarters in the miners' strike of 1912. And the Travellers was once the village mortuary. Both these two latter pubs date from the eighteenth century.

Near to Hemsworth is the Kinsley Hotel, a large Edwardian pub that for many years was the only house in Yorkshire owned by the Boddington Brewery of Manchester. Continued enquiries have failed to find out why this should be, as it was about thirty miles from the next nearest tied house.

LEEDS

'The busy Mart, the temperate Council Board. The patriotic voice of ancient Leeds.'
Anon

Leeds lays claim to the oldest surviving public house in England within its boundaries. Although there are several others from lesser counties also bidding for the title, the Bingley Arms at Bardsey on the eastern outposts of the city has excellent credentials.

The *Guinness Book of Records* says it is the oldest inhabited inn in the country, and there is a complete set of records detailing all the innkeepers and brewers from 1000 AD. Samson Ellis was the first recorded brewer and landlord in 953 AD. Ellis's family remained in control here until the late eighteenth century, when it was known as the Priests Inn. Later it was associated with Kirkstall Abbey, as it was used as a rest house for priests travelling between there and St Mary's in York. When the Ellis family left in 1780, the landowner Lord Bingley, who lived at nearby Bramham Park, changed the name to its present one. The original brewhouse stood until 1942 when it was destroyed during an ARP exercise. It used water from a nearby spring and supplied beer to an area of up to twelve miles away. Part of the centre of the building dates from the tenth century, but the two ends were added in 1738. The inn still contains two priest holes and an eighteenth century Dutch oven.

Located in a yard off Briggate in Leeds city centre, the Pack Horse could claim to have been in continuous business since 1615, but two years ago it closed for alterations and the subsequent rebuilding is on another site and in no way reflects the historic character of the former pub. It started life as the Nags Head, and was part of the estate of the Manor of Whitkirk which belonged to the Order of St John of Jerusalem — a Templar Cross on the front wall indicated this. During the eighteenth century it acquired the nickname of 'Slipin'. In 1750 a dancing academy was opened here and in later years — with four theatres nearby — it was a favourite with theatrical types. In the next yard is the Ship Inn, a Georgian pub that also attracted actors and musicians. The Wrens in Upper Briggate still retains a theatrical ambience. It is a favourite with members of Opera North, based at the Grand Theatre with which the pub has always been associated. Despite the birds on its sign it takes its name from Mr Wren, the first landlord, and is a rare survivor of the once-common method of naming pubs after their owners.

Barneys in Swan Street — formerly the White Swan — has the most tangible and lasting links with the theatre. It was built in the middle of the eighteenth century as a coaching inn. Above it is the City Palace of Varieties, opened as an extension to the pub in 1865 as 'Thornton's New Music Hall and Fashionable Lounge'. In 1897 a team of clog dancers were on the bill, one of which was Charlie Chaplin, the first of many famous stars to appear there. Filming of the BBC television programme *The Good Old Days* started there in 1953 under producer Barney Colehan, after whom the pub is now named. The programme was to continue for thirty years.

Briggate is the focal point of Leeds, and reflects its historic past with its yards, alleys and fashionable Victorian arcades, each of which had an inn or pub in them at one time. The best known of those remaining is Whitelocks in Turks Head Yard. This splendid tavern was first licensed in 1715. In 1880 it was bought by the Whitelock family and in 1886 rebuilt in its present form. Little has changed since then. It was frequented by the artistic and business community, and the Leeds Savage Club — a society of artists, writers and musicians — met there. It was founded by the eccentric Edmund Bogg, a Leeds picture framer, who was known as 'T' owd Chief' because of his idiosyncracy of wearing a Red Indian chief's headdress. Whitelocks was one of the first places in the city to have electric lighting and an electric clock. Ironically, at that time Charles Francis Tetley, grandson of Joshua Tetley and a Lord Mayor of Leeds, was offered a free trial of electricity in his Headingley home and refused it!

Whitelocks in Turks Head Yard in the 1940's. Betjeman called it 'the very heart of Leeds'.

John Betjeman enjoyed the atmosphere of Whitelocks. He described it as:

'…the Leeds equivalent of Fleet Street's Old Cheshire Cheese and far less self-conscious, and does a roaring trade. It is the very heart of Leeds.'

It calls itself the 'First City Luncheon Bar', and this function continues today. The yard, entered from either end, is long and narrow and this is reflected inside with the long marble-topped bar. Long-lost breweries are commemorated here — Joule and Son of Stone in Staffordshire, Vaux and Company of Macauley Street in Leeds — and on etched mirrors, soup and bread is offered for sale for a penny! The original trade mirrors are just one element of this grand pub with its art nouveau glasswork, cast iron tables fitting snugly into comfortable settles and the general ambience of a century ago when only dwarves were employed as waiters. It is, naturally enough, a listed building of historic and architectural interest.

The Old Kings Arms was in a building in Briggate close to Duncan Street that dated from the seventeenth century. It was the city's first coaching inn but established itself as the Kings Arms Tavern long before that. In 1760 it serviced the first regular service to the Swan with Two Necks in London — a journey which took four days — and later the Royal Mail services to the capital also left from here.

The magistrates held court here and the turnpike commissioners used the inn for their meetings, so it was significant when in 1753 a riot occurred which connected the two. Four men had been arrested for refusing to pay turnpike charges at Harewood Bridge and were being held at the Kings Arms. Fellow objectors tried to storm the place and managed to release one prisoner. As a result the army was called in, the mayor read the Riot Act and the troops fired a round of powder which only served to anger the mob even more. The soldiers then loaded with shot and opened fire. Eight men were killed immediately and forty more were injured, some of whom died later. The riots, which had been particularly prevalent in the Bradford area, then gradually died away. The Old Kings Arms ceased to be an inn in 1813 when it was converted to shops.

The Bull and Mouth on Briggate was named after a naval victory by Henry VIII. Further along was the Albion.

Another of Briggate's coaching inns was the Bull and Mouth, probably a corruption of 'Boulogne mouth' after Henry VIII defeated the French in that town's harbour. Coaching started there in 1800 and it was one of the busiest houses in Leeds. In 1831 a box was deposited there off the Duke of Leeds coach from Manchester marked: 'To the Revd. Mr. Geneste, Hull, per Selby packet. To be left until called for.' A curious servant opened the box to find two corpses in there. (This was, of course, the high period of body snatching.) The Bull and Mouth changed its name to the Grand Central Hotel in 1903, and after the Great War to the Victory Hotel. It was demolished in 1939 for the building of a large store.

The Alliance Vaults, better known as McConnells, was in Briggate near to Market Street. It was very popular and much missed even into present memory. There was nowhere to sit except on a few old barrels and much of the trade was in spirits. A speciality of the house was Ind Coope Old No 2 Ale which was only sold in half pints. An indication of its trade can be gauged from the fact that, during the 1930's, it sold more than 3,000 pints of beer a week — and this accounted for less than one third of its total sales!

There has probably been a pub on the site of the the Adelphi on Leeds Bridge, close to the Tetley Brewery, since before 1839, but the present building dates from the turn of the century. The name 'Adelphi' is probably a corruption of the Greek word for brothers, but as to why it is used as the name of a pub is uncertain. Possibly it means the comradeship of brothers who use an inn — the 'brotherhood of drinkers'. It stands on the southern side of Leeds Bridge on an imposing corner site, curving gracefully and displaying a granite facade to some effect. Above the entrance the landlord is noted as being 'licensed to brew' although it is many years since this was the case.

The Edwardian splendour of the Adelphi on Leeds Bridge.

The Adelphi has been used in recent years to recreate the custom of the brig and shot or brigshot — porridge, meat and ale sold to the cloth merchants for twopence in the seventeenth and eighteenth centuries. When Daniel Defoe wrote his *A Tour through the Whole Island of Great Britain* in 1724 he commented favourably upon the practice:

'Leeds is a large, wealthy and populous Town. It stands on the North Bank of the River AIRE, or rather on both sides of the River, for there is a large Suburb or Part of the Town on the South Side of the River, and the whole is joined by a stately and prodigiously strong Stone Bridge, so large and so wide, that formerly the Cloth Market was kept in neither Part of the Town, but on the very Bridge itself; and therefore the Refreshment given the Clothiers by the Inn-keepers is called the BRIGG-SHOT to this Day.'

Hidden away in the brewery complex behind the Adelphi is a former public house that has a very special place in the history of Tetleys. The Duke William was the first pub to be bought by the brewery in 1890 — much later than many of its competitors had moved into the tied trade. The pub closed in 1953, but remains intact with its original layout. In fact it dates back to the 1820's and was known as a popular overnight stop for bargees on the nearby Aire and Calder Navigation and the Leeds and Liverpool Canal. Tetleys paid £2,237 10s for it. In the same year the firm bought the Fleece at Farsley in west Leeds for £2,206 15s 5d and this pub remains open. A landlord of the Fleece, Frank Long, held the licence from 1901 to 1957. He recalled when he and his wife celebrated their golden wedding in 1953 that, at the start of his tenancy, beer cost threepence a pint and the pub was open from six in the morning until eleven at night.

The Garden Gate in Hunslet once stood on the main road from Leeds into Hunslet, but this has now been sealed off by an incong-ruous metal fence protecting the local Catholic church. It must rank as one of the finest examples of a Victorian public house in Yorkshire, if not in Britain. There are several pubs in Leeds in the Garden Gate mould, although it stands out clearly as not only the best original but the best preserved.

It was built originally in the 1820's, but it was not until 1849 that it was referred to by its present name, which probably derives from

The Garden Gate's opulent tap room has changed little since the turn of the century.

the market gardens in the area. (The nearby Gardeners Arms, a splendid unspoilt village inn, had a landlord at that time who combined his job with that of a market gardener.) In 1881 Edward Wilson bought what was described as:

'...all that plot, piece or part of land situate in Hunslet aforesaid adjoining upon the old highway leading from Leeds to Hunslet and known as Waterloo Road. Together with that messuage or Public House known as the Garden Gate Inn with the brew house, wash house, yard and appertenances thereto...'

In the late 1960's, with the city council anxious to redevelop the area, the future of the pub was most uncertain. Plans were put forward to demolish the whole area and rebuild it with houses, shops, churches, clubs and even a couple of pubs, one of them to replace the

Garden Gate. But the move had not escaped the notice of two trainee planners who lived in the nearby Hunslet Grange Flats. They were regulars in the pub, and they approached a local councillor who suggested that the development should be around the Garden Gate. As a result the pub and the nearby library were saved. Shortly afterwards it was listed as a building of special architectural interest.

Hunslet was — and to some extent remains — the industrial heart of Leeds. The Yorkshire Copper Works employed men in the foundry who had a reputation for heavy drinking, and occasionally contests were held to prove their prowess. One such took place in the Crooked Billet at Thwaite Gate. The Copper Works champion was set up against the star drinker from Coghlan's Forge. Eight quarts of ale were laid out for each drinker and the contest began. The Copper Works man saw off his own eight and then four of his opponent's to become a clear winner.

The Market Tavern is known to this day as 'the mad house'.

Opposite Cuthbert Brodrick's impressive town hall is a splendid building that was once known as the Jubilee Hotel. Mark Girouard in his book *Victorian Pubs* says it is the city's only genuine remaining gin palace, a species which he describes as the haunt of mainly the lower middle class. The Jubilee has an impressive five-storied pink terracotta facade with excellent art nouveau windows.

Behind the town hall stands the Victoria Family and Commercial Hotel, dating from 1864. It is a superb five-storied building which over many years has been a favourite hostelry for lawyers, musicians, journalists and politicians. Charles Pannell, Labour MP for Leeds West for twenty-five years and later a member of the House of Lords, said he always felt more at home in 'the Vic' than in any other pub. It was, he said, 'the most civilised of establishments'. It was built with the specific purpose of serving the magistrates' courts across the road, and this is remembered by a plaque placed there recently by the Civic Trust. One city centre pub that had more than its share of trouble in its time is the Market Tavern, close to the splendid Victorian Kirkgate Market. In the last century, fights were commonplace, along with drinking after time and good old-fashioned drunkenness. To this day the place is known as 'the mad house' but sadly it is due for demolition.

The Whip, tucked away in an alleyway off Duncan Street, is said to have sold more beer in its heyday between the wars than any other pub in Leeds — some 25,000 pints in a week. It was the classic city centre alehouse which catered for men only. Only within the last decade, and to comply with the law, were women's toilets installed.

Near to the railway station, the Scarbrough — note the spelling — is named after the man who built it and not the seaside town. It is on the site of the original Leeds Manor House, was first called the Kings Arms, and then took the name Scarbroughs Hotel. Dr John Simpson, a diarist who visited the place in 1825, called it '...the best house in Leeds by far'. The Prince of Wales and his entourage were accomodated in 1857 on their way to Harewood House, and when the Wood family were the landlords around the turn of the century the pub was popular with theatricals. In 1890 George Broadbent was a top rugby player, playing for the Leeds Parish Church team (predecessors of the present Leeds club). He was also employed at the Scarbrough as a waiter, and the landlord advertised his sporting prowess to attract custom.

Leeds has several pubs which are reputedly haunted. At the Golden Lion in North Street, it was said that a gentleman in top hat and tails and an elderly lady with her hair in ringlets were often seen. The view was that they were possibly the couple who ran the pub in the early nineteenth century and who were reluctant to leave. The pub was demolished in 1970. Across the city in Kippax, a former landlord of the Old Tree also keeps a friendly presence by walking through the bar to the back of the house where his bedroom used to be. Again it is said that he is loath to leave the pub he loved so well. But he has been mischievous too, turning off the jukebox on occasions and upsetting containers in the cellar. There is a slightly more sinister spectre at the Royal Hotel in Armley. There are claims that a grey lady has been seen, thought to have been the mistress of a former landlord murdered by him in 1858.

The northern exits from the city were once thickly laid with inns, taverns and, in particular, beerhouses. North Street, which led to the Wetherby and Harrogate turnpikes, had eleven pubs in the 1850's, but now only two are left. The Eagle Tavern is a fine Georgian building and yet another pub which is said to be haunted. A friendly 'spirit' has taken up residence in room seven on the top floor. No-one claims to have seen it, but a presence has been felt by people staying in the room and all say that they have had no difficulty in sleeping afterwards. The present landlord believes it may say something for the strength of the Timothy Taylors ale that he sells!

It was in North Street at the North Tavern where the hoary old tale was told of a man being thrown out of the pub's three doors within half an hour by the landlord, one Harry Tyler. 'How many pubs in North Street do you keep, Tyler?', asked the puzzled drunk.

In nearby Chapeltown Road until 1982 stood the Roscoe Inn, the city's last beerhouse. Only in 1976 was its licence amended to allow wines and spirits to be sold. Its other claim to fame was that it was 'the

The Roscoe in Chapeltown. A much missed pub.

cradle of Irish music' in Leeds. Not only did the Roscoe have Irish licensees for the last forty-six years of its life, it was also a haven for the Irish community — being known as 'the labour exchange' — and consequently for its music. At times, traditional music could be heard live in one room, on the jukebox in another and on television in a third. When the West Yorkshire County Council issued its plans to demolish the pub to make way for an elaborate road scheme, some 326 customers including Eric Atkinson, the Lord Mayor of Leeds, and the local Member of the European Parliament, Derek Enright, signed a petition calling for its retention. A public inquiry was held but the inspector agreed with the council. A plaque to 'a dearly loved pub' lies in the middle of what is now known as the Sheepscar Intersection.

The Skinners Arms in Buslingthorpe is a 1920's pub which replaced one that stood opposite and dated from around 1800. Its name comes from the leather industry of the area — which still exists — and when the present pub was built it was claimed that it was the only one in Leeds which had its own armorial emblem. It was known as 'T' Treacle Pot' for reasons which now seem lost in the mist of memories, but would no doubt be recalled by former landlord Walter Watson, who remained in active charge of the place until his death at the age of eighty-five, said at the time to be the oldest licensee in Leeds.

Chapel Allerton in North Leeds was once a thriving village in its own right. But, unlike many others which have been submerged by the city, it has retained the village atmosphere with village pubs. On the main road which was once the Harrogate turnpike is the Mex-borough Arms, formerly called the Bowling Green Inn and dating back to the early eighteenth century. It claims to have been the venue for the first cricket match in Yorkshire in 1757 and the Reverend J Ismay, who visited the village in 1767, wrote in his diary:

'There is a very good inn at ye Bowling Green and excellent accomodation. Three clubs are held at this place, viz: one for bowling, another for cricket and a third which is called Lascelles club.'

The name was changed during the nineteenth century, when it was described as 'a squat whitewashed house beside the depot for the horse tram service'. The present building dates from 1911 and the bowling green has now gone to be replaced by a car park.

The Regent, which was almost certainly named after the Prince Regent, has changed little since the early nineteenth century when it was built. The nearby Nags Head has had several changes in interior style since its origins in the mid-eighteenth century, but its fabric is untouched, with a mounting stone and a serving window.

The village no longer has a swan amongst its pubs. The Black Swan was in Woodland Lane at the entrance to what is now a public park. It later became a farmhouse but was partly demolished in the 1950's. The White Swan in Well Lane had a chequered history. It lost its licence in 1867, possibly because of rowdiness, and turned full circle to become a teetotal social club — one of the first of the 'British Workman's Public Houses' — with a sign that bore the inscription:

'A Public House without the drink
Where men may read, and smoke, and think
Then sober home return;
A stepping stone this house you'll find,
Come leave your rum and beer behind
And truer pleasures learn.'

It sold drinks that imitated the more famous alcoholic ones: 'Winterine' was the temperance wine, 'Anti-Burton' was the beer and aerated milk the champagne!

Otley, straddling the River Wharfe, has many historic values, particularly amongst its inns and public houses. It is another town with its pubs listed in story form on a much sought-after postcard written by Dick Sumner:

'Having an hour to spend in Otley the other evening I thought I would have a ramble around the town, and my attention was immediately attracted by a beautiful "Summer Cross" upon which "Three Horse Shoes" were nailed, guarded by a "Red Lion" which stood near a "Fountain" where a groom named "George" wearing a "Blue Bell" in his coat who came from a "Manor House" called the "Wharfedale" was giving a "White Horse", a "Bay Horse" and a "Black Horse" a drink; whilst a handsome "White Swan" "New Inn" the water was swimming gracefully about.

Turning round I saw a "Wheatsheaf" standing under the shade of a splendid "Royal Oak" which sheltered the "Leeds House". Hearing a shout I looked up and saw a man who had stolen a "Rose and Crown" bearing the stamp of the "Queens Head" running across the "Bowling Green" pursued by a crowd of people and a butcher with a "Black Bull". He tried to effect a "Junction" with his mate, a conjurer who was juggling with two "Cross Pipes" and a "Cock and Bottle" but failing in his attempt ran straight into the "Masons Arms" who was coming out of the "Dramshop" with a heavy "Woolpack" on his shoulders made from the "Fleece" of a prize sheep; and with the sound of "The Ring o' Bells" ringing merrily in my ears, I retired to rest aided by the light of the "Half Moon" and the evening "Star".'

The Black Bull in the market square is a magnificent little-altered tavern which retains an atmosphere reminiscent of medieval times: low and long, white-rendered and with a proud sign which, like many others in the immediate area, reflects the rural and agrarian position of the town. In 1648 a party of Cromwell's Ironsides are said to have called there for refreshment and drank the tavern dry.

The main door to the Black Bull is medieval if not original, yet solid and impressive, whilst inside is a stone fireplace — probably medieval — as well as a beautifully-preserved bread oven, with its original arched brickwork still intact. In its yard are stables, a water pump and a stone staircase. Much of the Black Bull is eighteenth century, but there is ample evidence that some parts date from even earlier, when it was two buildings.

Manor Square has several fine buildings in it, including what is now Barclays Bank but which was formerly the Royal White Horse Hotel. It was first built in the eighteenth century as a coaching inn, and was rebuilt in 1865 when Albert Walker, of the Otley family of printers, wrote a song entitled *New White Horse is Rising Fast*. It received the prefix 'Royal' after a visit by Prince Arthur, the Duke of Connaught, in 1876. The proclamation of the death of King George VI was read from the balcony of the hotel in 1952. It closed in 1973.

The Black Horse Hotel has a datestone of 1901, although there was an earlier inn here that was the starting point for coaches running between Otley and York through Harewood and Tadcaster. Through an imposing archway there is an excellently-preserved stable yard now used as garaging. The Black Horse is at the entrance to Kirkgate, which in the eighteenth and nineteenth centuries was thickly laid with taverns and beerhouses.

The Bowling Green Inn in Bondgate is dated 1757, but this relates to its original purpose when it was the town's courthouse. It later became the assembly rooms where dances, concerts and public meetings took place; it was also used as a school and a chapel. It became an inn in 1825, and used to issue its own beer tokens. These were common in many businesses, but proliferated in public houses around 1850 after the 1845 Gaming Act had made gambling for money illegal on licensed premises. The name of the pub or its owner was on one side and on the reverse was the value, ranging from a halfpenny to a shilling. Apart from gambling, they were given in return for admission to pub entertainments and sporting facilities such as bowling greens, and could then be exchanged for drink and tobacco in the pub.

In the middle of Queen Victoria's reign, a man from Otley called William Parkinson made a remark that 100 years later resulted in a pub changing its name. High to the north of Otley on Newall Carr Side is the Spite, a stone-built pub on the end of a short terrace that was built in 1783. However, it was 1852 before it became a pub, then known as the Roebuck. The following year two cottages at the other end of the terrace were also licensed and took the name of the Travellers Inn.

The relationship between the two pubs appears to have been somewhat fraught, and came to a head because of Mr Parkinson. He walked up the hill from Otley on most days and always drank in the Travellers — until the fateful day he decided to call in at the Roebuck. He stayed for about an hour and then moved on to the neighbouring house. But the landlady of the Travellers had seen him and she bawled him out, telling him to go back to where he had just been drinking.

He returned to the Roebuck, somewhat flustered, saying: 'There's

The Spite at Otley. Its name has an unusual tale behind it.

nowt but spite and malice up here.' From that day on the Roebuck was nicknamed the Spite and the Travellers was known as the Malice. In 1884 the Travellers closed down, but the Spite lived on, although its official name was still the Roebuck. When new tenants took over in 1980 they were confused by the fact that both names were in evidence on the pub. The magistrates were unhappy too, and wanted one name or the other. So, about 100 years after Mr Parkinson drank at the Roebuck, it officially became the Spite.

The Robin Hood is the oldest pub in Yeadon, probably dating from the early eighteenth century. It stands on the green and was the favourite place for receptions following weddings at Guiseley parish church. In the mid-nineteenth century, records show that after the wedding '…single men would gallop their horses from Swaine Hill to Thomas Townsend's Public House on the Green, the winner receiving a tankard of ale'.

The White Cross at Guiseley is a good example of a pub's name becoming the established name of the immediate area. Even the world-famous Harry Ramsden's, the nation's largest fish and chip shop which stands opposite, is usually said to be 'at the White Cross'. The pub was originally built in the eighteenth century as a coaching inn strategically located at the junctions of roads from Otley and Ilkley to Leeds and Bradford. Up to 1930 it was in two different licensing districts, with the boundary running through the middle of the pub, and time was called in one bar half an hour before the other.

The history of the pubs of Horsforth is well documented in the excellent booklet *The Inns, Taverns and Public Houses of Horsforth* by Christopher Townsley. There have been at least twenty-five pubs in Horsforth at one time or another. Of these, fourteen remain and all except one of these have their origins in the nineteenth century or earlier. The oldest is the Old Kings Arms on the green, for which the earliest references to it as an inn are in 1749. The present facade dates from 1879 — evidence of this can be clearly seen above the front door — but this conceals parts of the older building which are still in place. The magistrates met here and, appropriately, the village stocks were located just outside.

The Queens Arms in Long Row is thought to be the oldest building in Horsforth in use as a public house. It was built in the early part of the seventeenth century, and the first recorded landlord was John Longfellow in 1781. He was a cloth weaver and could well have been related, albeit distantly, to the poet Henry Wadsworth Longfellow. William Longfellow, the great-great-great-grandfather of the American nineteenth century poet, emigrated in 1676 from Horsforth to the New World and was also a cloth weaver. It is also interesting that the smithy in Longfellow's poem *The Village Blacksmith* is reputed to be in nearby Calverley. He also wrote a long series of poems, *Tales of a Wayside Inn,* in which '...the Red Horse prances on the sign...'.

At Calverley there is a pub which has its origins in the seventeenth century. A lintel inside the Thornhill Arms bears the date 1673 along with the initials WC and FC. At one time it framed the pub's front door, which was probably several feet behind the present one. This good-looking former coaching house was once called the Leopard, probably a heraldic reference to the weaving industry of the area (the crest of the Weavers' Company bears the heads of three leopards).

In the fiercely independent town of Pudsey — between Leeds and Bradford — the Park is one of the oldest pubs, dating from 1734. It was once called the Pavilion, recalling its use by local cricket clubs who played opposite in what is now a public park. During the early nineteenth century it was listed as the New Inn. It retains a fire insurance mark high on its superb frontage and, at one time, a cast-iron black cat sat on the roof to bring good luck to the house.

The Park, which also claims a lady ghost, is rivalled by Golden Lion as the town's oldest. One claim for its origins is two years before the Park, another for ten years later. In the yard of the Golden Lion an engraved stone reads: 'This is a mean Gable End betwixt Thomas Wood and Daniel Moore AD 1810.'

In Morley, the Morley Dashers takes its name from the 'dashers', piece-workers who carried finished pieces of cloth from Morley to Leeds and dashed back for more. On the road from Morley to Batley you will find the Needless, originally called the Cardigan Arms. It was one of three pubs on this road and the magistrates, who can be seen conferring on its present day sign, decided that two were enough; the middle one was 'needless'. But it continued and the name prevails. It is also one of many pubs in Yorkshire where Dick Turpin was said to have downed his last drink.

On Churwell Hill there are three pubs — the Commercial, the Old Golden Fleece and the New Inn — which are known to the locals as 'top 'ole', 'middle 'ole' and 'bottom 'ole'. (''Ole' or possibly ''oil' means hole — as in watering hole). Bobby Peel, the Yorkshire and England cricketer, was the landlord of the Commercial after he ceased to play the first class game in 1897. During his career he took 1,500 wickets for his county and 102 in 20 Test matches, all against Australia. But his predeliction for ale led to the end of his cricket career and his subsequent entry into the licensed trade. He was sacked by the formidable Yorkshire captain, Lord Hawke, during a season in which the two of them had broken the Yorkshire eighth wicket

Bobby Peel, Yorkshire and
England cricketer, was
landlord of the Commercial or
the 'top 'ole' at Churwell.

partnership record with a score of 262 against Warwickshire, of which
Peel scored 210 not out. Later in the season Bobby celebrated another
fine performance with a booze-up of heroic proportions, so the
following day he was still considerably hung over. He commenced
bowling by running towards the sight screen and his fellow players had
to turn him round. This was too much for his lordship, who forbade
him to play for Yorkshire again.

West Leeds has more in keeping with the urban West Riding than
with the city of Leeds. The village pub remains an institution, with
the Old Unicorn in Bramley as one of the best examples. It is 200 years
old, solidly built in stone quarried at nearby Bramley Falls, standing
high above the village centre and next to the church. Its near
neighbour was the Cardigan Arms, a seventeenth century inn which
was the terminus of a coach service from Bramley to the Griffin Hotel
in Leeds.

At the other end of Bramley Town Street is the Barley Mow, first
built in the eighteenth century but much altered since then. The

Bennett family kept it from 1868 to 1920, and in January 1918 it was noted in the records of the Melbourne Brewery that:

'Young Bennett came to the office on behalf of his mother and offered us the house for £12,000. He was invited to guess again. Premises consist of an inn, 5 cottages and a football field and a brewhouse but no brewing for several years.'

In 1920 it was sold to Armley Brewery for £12,000. The football ground, which took its name from the pub, was used for many years by the Bramley Rugby League Club. Teams changed in the pub, which had an extension on match days.

Armley is more a suburb than a village, with a fair share of pubs of all types. But the Nelson is its most interesting, mainly because of the man who was its licensee for more than fifty-six years. Samuel Ledgard took over the inn from his father, William, in 1896 and kept it until his death at the age of seventy-seven in 1952. He married twice and was the father of eleven children. Samuel Ledgard was, to use an overworked cliché, a legend in his own lifetime. The Nelson was the last homebrew pub in Leeds and in the 1920's, when most others were closing down, he expanded his brewery where he produced black beer, pale ale and home-brewed extra stout. But it was as a pioneer of motorbus transport that he was best known, becoming one of the largest independent road passenger transport operators in the country. After buying his first vehicle in 1906 he started catering at race meetings in Yorkshire and later he moved into general haulage, quarrying and farming. In 1930 he bought another pub, the Kings Arms at Tong, but ran the whole business from his home and office at the Nelson in Armley. Brewing ceased there when he died.

Under the shadow of Armley Jail is the Albion, a pub well-known to thousands of youngsters as it was used as the basis for the model pub on OO gauge model railway sets. It started life in the 1860's as two shops, one of which was used as a beerhouse and became the Fleece Inn in 1873. The other shop is recorded as becoming the Albion Hotel around 1886. After the Great War the justices began to refuse to renew licences of uneconomic pubs, particularly those in areas which

The Albion in Armley was formerly two pubs.

appeared to have too many. The Fleece and the Albion were obvious targets but a hint was dropped to the owners, Walkers of Warrington, that a merger of the two would receive favourable consideration. The alterations were considerable and received praise from the magistrates when completed in 1921. The impressive fascia sign board is still there today, but was covered over for many years after Walkers sold the new Albion to Tetleys for £9,000 in 1925.

The actress Sarah Siddons used to stay at the Star and Garter at Kirkstall Bridge when appearing in Leeds. This eighteenth century pub takes its name from the Order of the Garter — the star is part of the insignia. It is said that Mrs Siddons stayed there when she performed at the Leeds Theatre in Hunslet Lane in 1807. The date may be doubtful, for after a stormy appearance there in 1786 she told the rowdy audience: 'Farewell ye brutes, and for ever, I trust; ye shall never torture me again!'

The Cardigan Arms in Kirkstall has connections with the Charge of the Light Brigade.

The Cardigan Arms in Burley has origins back into the eighteenth century, but the present building dates from 1895. The Earls of Cardigan and the Brudenell family owned vast tracts of land in Leeds — in particular in the Headingley, Burley and Kirkstall areas — and it was a common practice for a pub to be named after the family on whose estates it stood. The Brudenells, and in particular the Fifth Earl of Cardigan who led the disastrous Charge of the Light Brigade, had not been good landlords, and when the pub was sold in 1890 it was so run down that the magistrates considered refusing a licence. They granted a provisional one when a new owner submitted plans for rebuilding, and confirmed it when he completed it in much the form seen today, with its unchanged interior and fine facade with an unusual 'missing' window.

Headingley's New Inn must have been quite rural when it was first built, as other buildings in the area are much later in construction. It is a pleasant stone building, with some splendid glass etched with the name of 'Bentley's Yorkshire Breweries' of Woodlesford. The name New Inn often relates to an old pub and can have several meanings, the most common being that it had replaced another on the same site; or it may simply be the latest, or newest, to be built in a village or area. A number date from Queen Elizabeth's time after she pronounced on the poor quality of accomodation available for travellers. Suprisingly there are fifteen New Inns in Leeds, and at least another nine have closed or vanished. (It is easily the city's most popular pub name.) They range from those built in the eighteenth century — such as the one at Barwick-in-Elmet — to a 1930's roadhouse like the one in Scarcroft. But anyone entering the Headingley pub of that name with the hope of having a beer on the slate should take warning from the dummy clock above the front door which proclaims: 'No Tick'!

BRADFORD

'...Bruddersford [Bradford] is generally held to be an ugly city; and so I suppose it is; but it always seemed to me to have the kind of ugliness that could not only be tolerated but often enjoyed; it was grim but not mean.'

J B Priestley

Bradford often appears to be under the shadow of its next door neighbour Leeds. But it is a proud city, and whilst it does not have the fine stately city centre pubs of its neighbour, it does have some excellent houses, well-preserved and projecting a dignity not often found in provincial cities. Like Leeds it is essentially a Victorian city, with its rapid growth coming from the development of the textile industry. In the nineteenth century its population rose from 6,000 to almost 250,000.

Its strong liberal tradition is obvious as far back as the fourteenth century in the attitudes displayed towards drinking. Drunkenness was not regarded as a misdemeanour, nor were any restrictions placed on landlords as to the hours in which they opened. Anyone could open an inn or beerhouse with the sanction of the manor court and on payment of one shilling.

There were restrictions, however, on the quality of liquor brewed, and this had to be tasted before being offered for sale by a suitably-qualified person, the aptly named 'ale taster'. At one time the man in the post in Bradford was the appropriately named Thomas Nut-browne, who was also an innkeeper or 'hostiler'. By the end of the eighteenth century there were more than fifty inns and about thirty alehouses in Bradford. By 1850 the number of inns had doubled and the beerhouses had multiplied fivefold, the former as the result of economic and social changes and the latter mainly because of the 1830 Beerhouse Act. But the standards in Victorian times were not high, and the premises were not well-conducted. One Vicar of Bradford, John Crosse, found it necessary to present a memorial to the licensing justices objecting to licences being granted to ten of them. The situation worsened, and a special committee was set up in 1849 to inquire into the moral condition of the town.

The beerhouses in particular were seen as dens of iniquity. The report of the committee confirmed this:

'...many are notoriously bad...haunts of the vilest characters and scenes of perpetual drunkenness and debauchery...some are in fact brothels under another name.'

Some provided music, and this upset the authorities. In fact the chief constable had threatened landlords with the loss of their licences if it continued, but the beerhouses continued to prosper until the requirement of a justices' licence was reimposed in 1869. Two years later the police were expressing some satisfaction at the way licensed premises were run, but they had used the new laws to close down many of the badly-conducted ones.

When William Scruton wrote his *Pen and Pencil Pictures of Old Bradford* in 1880 he referred to the Church Steps Inn as the oldest in the town. As its name implies, it was close to what is now the cathedral and was an 'indispensible accessory for baptisms, weddings, funerals, etc'. Its most attractive part was said to be the ginnel at the rear leading from the steps to Church Bank. Churchgoers used the pub, and it was also a meeting-place for bellringers and the churchwardens. On the 3rd February each year the Church Steps Society dined in commemoration of the Saint's Day of Bishop Blaize, the patron saint of woolcombers. (There was a Bishop Blaize Inn in Westgate, and it is a name still to be found in Yorkshire, including an historic one in Richmond in the North Riding.) Along with the adjoining grammar school the Church Steps was demolished in 1887 to build Bradford's General Post Office.

The oldest surviving public house in Bradford is thought to be the Jacobs Well Tavern in Kent Street in the city centre. It was built as a water house probably in the early eighteenth century. The Bowling Green Hotel in Market Street was a seventeenth century building, and when it was rebuilt in 1750 it was known as the 'best inn in town'. It had a bowling green at the rear, Wesley and Whitfield preached at

The Church Steps, where the General Post Office now stands, was 'an indispensible accesory for baptisms, weddings, funerals, etc'.

The Bowling Green Hotel was heavily involved with the political life of the city.

the front, political meetings were held and travelling theatres performed there. It advertised 'unlimited accomodation for man and beast'. This open space before the hotel was shared with the Sun in Ivegate. Both were 'yellow houses', meaning they supported the Liberal party, and important public meetings were held there, particularly after the 1832 Reform Act which vastly expanded the franchise. The Bowling Green Hotel was demolished in 1850.

The Sun was noted in its day for its great dancing assemblies, but it was as the result of a public meeting there in 1766 that its name is best remembered. On the 2nd July in that year, John Hustler, a wool trader from Bradford, and John Longbottom, a Halifax engineer, proposed the idea of a canal crossing the Pennines to link Leeds with Liverpool. The enthusiastic and well-attended meeting supported them and an Act of Parliament received the royal assent in 1770. Work commenced at once on the 127 mile long canal — which took until 1816 to complete.

Another political inn was the Talbot Hotel in Kirkgate. Though its origins were in the middle of the seventeenth century, it became the headquarters of the local Tories in the early nineteenth century. It was a 'blue house', and one room was kept for leading members of the party. The pub was said to have 'a select and snobby air'. It was a coaching house and the well-known Union coach called here on its journeys between Leeds and Kendal. It was rebuilt in 1880 and the impressive wooden dog sign — the talbot being an extinct breed of hunting dog — was taken to Walton Hall near Wakefield. It became the headquarters of the Bradford Rugby Club, and was the venue for a number of secret meetings prior to the crisis in 1895 when clubs broke away from the English Rugby Union to form their own organisation that was to become the Rugby League.

The Old Red Ginn in Bowling Old Lane became the headquarters of Bradford Northern after the split. It was first recorded as an inn in 1735 and took its name from a form of hoist used in the colleries of the area. (The spelling may have been to distinguish it from the drink.) It was knocked down in 1968 and a new pub was built close by.

There had been drinking on the site of the Queen in Bridge Street since the middle of the eighteenth century, although the pub that carried that name was only built in 1775, and it was probably seventy years later before it took the name from Queen Victoria. Up to its demolition in 1964 it had been the haunt of commercials, with its upstairs dining room providing good value lunches. A new pub has been built on the site.

Bradford's first flower show was held at the New Inn in Tyrrel Street in 1827. It became the headquarters of the Bradford Florist Society, which offered a pair of silver sugar tongs as the prize for the 'best scarlet bizarre' and copper kettles for every other class winners. Admission to the show was one shilling. It was built in 1810 as a private house, and on becoming an inn the magistrates used it for their court. In 1840 the uniquely-named Querical Society started to meet there. They were a band of men anxious to improve their knowledge of the world, and all within and without it. The New Inn also had extensive stabling, and its big yard was the venue for a regular pig market.

The improvement commissioners met at the White Lion in Kirkgate, a pub which had its origins in the 1730's. It was rebuilt in the Victorian era but demolished to allow offices to be built in 1960.

At the Three Horse Shoes in Tyrell Street a one-time landlord, Jesse Clayton, was also a shoesmith so his wife, Eunice, was regarded as — and eventually became — the licensee. She was a hard woman, but one with a heart of gold. She had a room for what she called the 'dobby weyvers' — the rest entered it at their peril. And she stopped any drunk attempting to enter the house by claiming she had 'bother eniff with her own drink without other fowk's'.

The Nags Head in Kirkgate was an old inn that was closed in 1865 when the moral view of the time was against such places. It had a dram shop, a small bar which specialised in selling spirits. It was a Scottish tradition, but one occasionally found in Yorkshire pubs, particularly in Bradford and Sheffield. They were brash and brightly-lit rooms, the forerunners of the gin palace. But their clientele was questionable; a local journalist, James Burnley, wrote of dram shops as being 'a mass of vice and wretchedness, profligacy and despair'.

In Westgate was the Bulls Head, in front of which was the bull ring where bull-baiting took place. It was a meeting place for merchants and woolmen, and the first Bradford club met there for whom the landlady, Mrs Duckit, made 'genuine rum punch'. It also had a great musical reputation: the Choral Society rehearsed here on the Tuesday on or before the full moon so that the musicians from the countryside could find their way home. (The town's first concert hall was in the Bermondsey Hotel, later named the London Hotel.)

Bradford Cricket Club was born in the Hope and Anchor in Bank Street, and other inns and pubs became the regular venues for meetings of various organisations: the Manningham Angling Club had its headquarters at the Woolpack in Whetley Hill; and Bradford Bicycle Club set out on their perambulations from the Thorncliffe in Manningham Lane.

Amongst the town's trade unions, the dyers met at the Exchange in City Road, the plumbers at the Pack Horse in Westgate and the Old Crown in Ivegate hosted the saddlers (the latter was also the venue for a music hall).

In Westgate, the Angel was once kept by William Lister who doubled as a chimney sweep. His sign read:

'Who lives here? Who do you think?
Major Lister, give him a drink.
Give him a drink, for why?
Because when he's sweeping
He's always dry.'

Bradford has celebrated heroes such as Lord Clyde — who relieved Lucknow in 1857 — with a pub in Thornton Road; the Admiral Nelson is in Manchester Road; and the General Grant in White Abbey Road is named after Ulysses S Grant, commander of the Union forces in the American Civil War and twice President of the United States. The Church Hill is on Church Bank but has displayed a portrait of the former prime minister, and Gladstone can claim to have had no less than four pubs named after him in Bradford.

The temperance movement flourished in Bradford during the mid-nineteenth century; starting in 1830 it developed with the formation of the Band of Hope in 1851 to have 21,000 members by 1883. The Bradford Coffee Tavern Company, whilst not aligned to the movement, attracted people sworn off alcoholic drinks and had twenty-three branches at its zenith. The working men's club movement started in Bradford in 1860 with clubs that were drink-free, but other clubs that followed attracted the middle and upper classes and political and social groups, and provided drink. The Liberal Club was started in 1871 and the Conservative Club in 1878. Prior to these had been the Union Club, the Bradford Club, and the Schiller Verein in Little Germany for the many German merchants in the town.

Coaching reached Bradford rather later than other towns in Yorkshire. The first services, in 1683, ran from London to York, and passengers for Leeds and Bradford had to travel on horseback from Ferrybridge or York. Later the town was swept up in the riots against the turnpikes. Men dressed up as women, blacked up their faces and became known as 'Rebeccas'. When trouble was afoot the cry was: 'Rebecca has gone out to sweep'. There were attacks on several toll houses in the area. In 1753 a mob of several hundred attacked and burnt the ones at Tyersall, Newall Hall and Wibsey. But, following the attacks at Harewood and the deaths in Leeds when the military opened fire, the riots ceased.

The White Swan stood where the Swan Arcade now is, and was one of Bradford's smaller coaching inns. The Highflyer also called there — a coach which has left its mark with a pub of that name in Leeds Road — and a landlord, John Bradford, was its coachman. Another landlord called Fox had his name proudly displayed under the sign of the swan. This puzzled a lady from Wibsey, fresh into town. 'Wha, that's nivver a fox i' this world', she said, 'it's nowt but a gooise!'

By 1846 the railway had reached Bradford, and the coaching days were at an end. The most lasting example of the railway hotel in Bradford is the Midland, which opened in 1890 as an integral part of the Midland Railway Station. The idea had first been suggested in 1874, and when completed this five storey, sixty bedroom hotel cost £1,000,000.

The Midland Hotel, where Sir Henry Irving (inset) died in 1905.

Its greatest claim to fame is that amongst the many famous actors and stage stars who have stayed there over the years, the most famous, Sir Henry Irving, died there in 1905. He had been appearing as Becket at the Theatre Royal, and when he arrived at the hotel in a poorly state he was helped to a small room off the lobby, where he sat down and died. Seymour Hicks, the producer and farceur, took on the detective mantle to trace the chair in which Irving expired. He eventually found it because a hotel servant had marked the initials 'HI' under the seat. 'I knew Henry Irving was a great man, sir', he said with remarkable understatement. Hicks bought the chair and presented it to the Garrick Club in London.

The George in Market Street was also favoured by theatricals, the artistic community and the literati. Branwell Brontë graced it — as he did so many other inns and taverns of the area — and Charles Dickens, who knew and wrote so well about the English inn, stayed here in 1854 on his first visit to Bradford when he read his *Christmas Carol* at St George's Hall.

The Cock and Bottle on Barkerend Road. 'Cock' means a spigot or tap.

The 'classic Victorian pub', according to Paul Jennings in his first-class pamphlet *Inns and Pubs of Old Bradford,* is the Cock and Bottle on Barkerend Road and it is difficult to disagree with him. First references to it can be found in 1747 in one of those quaint pieces of local legislation by which the Lord of the Manor of Bradford gave permission to a Manchester woman, Hannah Beswick, to leave it to whoever she pleased in her will. The tenancy, of what was then described as '...house, barn and buildings thereto...in Barker-End Bradford...also that cottage...and also that close of land known as the Toad-hole', was known as a 'copyhold' property, and as these were moving out of fashion in the previous century it does indicate that the site has a long history.

In 1643 during the Civil War it was said that the wife of Sir Thomas Fairfax, the Roundhead commander, was captured there during the second siege of Bradford by Royalist troops. One tale — without any foundation — says she escaped down an underground passage which led either to the nearby seventeenth century Paper Hall or to Bradford Cathedral. But this does lead on to a number of widely-spread stories that there was a passageway from the Cock and Bottle leading to somewhere. Chris Scargill, who has researched the history of the pub, examined the supposed passage entrance in the cellars and found it to be simply a hole knocked into the cellar wall, and the cathedral authorities denied the existence of a tunnel at their end when the *Telegraph and Argus* investigated it in 1977.

The possibilities are that there was an alehouse on this site in 1773, although there have been several partial and complete rebuildings since then. The name Cock and Bottle was taken about 1822, and is thought to mean that it sold both draught and bottled beers (the word 'cock' meaning a spigot or tap). The frontage and interior were rebuilt in 1862 and it has remained largely unchanged since then, the only major difference being the present music room replacing a kitchen and bar parlour.

The myriad of small rooms remain, with their splendid etched glass, mirrors and woodwork. The main bar contains lockable boxes which were used by merchants to keep their samples in — or their top hats when they were drinking — and one compartment housed an antique central heating system. It is another Bradford pub that has theatrical connections: the great Florrie Ford drank there when she appeared in the town. The attached eighteenth century brewhouse continued operating until 1927, making it one of the last home brew houses in Bradford.

The Spotted House in Manningham Lane probably relates to the 'House at the Spot' mentioned in 1504 during the reign of Henry VIII, although rebuilding has gone on apace since then. During the nineteenth century it boasted a bowling green, tennis courts and a swimming pool. J B Priestley lived nearby and drank there, and later wrote affectionately of it as 'a haunt of rare souls'. Priestley was known to enjoy his drink and love the ambience of the public house — in particular the George at Hubberholme at the top of Wharfedale. (His remains are in the churchyard of that village.)

Another historic suburban inn is the Lower George in Whetley Hill where the poor law commissioners met and distributed their dole. It just reaches back into the seventeenth century — records show an inn there in 1699 — although the present building dates from sixty years later.

The tiny village of Mountain on the road from Brighouse to Denholme is the home for a very historic pub. Ye Old Raggalds Inn started life in the eighteenth century as a farmhouse selling ale, and is best summed up by Alfred J Brown in his book *Four Boon Fellows:*

> 'Now here's to the Inn with the rollicking name
> And the stiffest of Sack and the fattest of game!
> O here's to the inn that is hoary with fame —
> Old Raggalds'! Old Raggalds'!'

In the mid-nineteenth century the Raggalds was a place famed for its gambling and illicit drinking, which presumably meant drinking through the night as licensing hours in those days were most liberal. The village is isolated — despite being on a main road — standing 1,200 feet above sea level, so the attentions of the police would be well telegraphed. Big gambling schools also took place at the nearby Withens, which was famed for its cock fighting and knurr and spell. (Known as 'poor man's golf' and played by hitting a projectile with a club or stick, it still remains popular around Halifax.) The Withens, which stands at 1,392 feet and is the highest pub in the West Riding, was built in 1862 for quarryworkers. It also earns a rhyme in Brown's book:

> 'A lonely inn, the Withens' Inn
> Atop o' the moor!
> And O for the joy of a pint within
> Its oaken door!'

The Blue Pig at Fagley is tucked away on the city boundary and its gents' toilets are actually in Pudsey. The name comes after a labourer cleaning the pig sties added a dolly blue to the whitewash, as his mother did with the weekly wash. Having cleaned down the building he gave the pigs a good scrubbing — with the consequent results!

One of the longest serving pubs in the Tetley estate is the Gardeners Arms at Eccleshill. They bought it in 1895, although it originated in the eighteenth century when it was known as the Smiling Mule — a name to which it recently reverted.

In Apperley Bridge the sixteenth century George and Dragon alongside the River Aire is stone-built around an oak tree. An extra wing was added in the early eighteenth century. The three pubs of Thackley are all nineteenth century. The oldest is the Shoulder of Mutton which dates from 1800 and was a main road coaching inn. The Great Northern, a mid-Victorian pub, stood next to a station that closed in the 1930's. And the Commercial, tucked away in the village, is reputedly haunted.

On the canal at Shipley the Bull Hotel, formerly the Bull and Dog, has loading wharves and at one time provided stabling for tow horses. The Branch was once a coaching house with the name of the Coach and Horses. The mid-nineteenth century Oddfellows Hall is one of several with this name taken from the friendly society that met there. The Old Glen House at the top of the Shipley Glen Victorian tramway is in a 400 year old former farmhouse and was at one time a temperance hotel.

In Wrose, the Bold Privateer was named after George, the third Earl of Cumberland, who owned the village. Baildon's oldest pub is the Angel, on the crossroads in the town centre. It was the venue for the manor courts in medieval days.

The Old White Horse in Bingley can trace its history back to the thirteenth century. It still displays the double cross sign to indicate its former ownership by the Knights of St John, who had many properties in the area. It stands on the old main road along with the Fleece; both were coaching inns, two of many in this strategic location between Leeds and Bradford to the east and Keighley and Skipton to the west.

The Fleece still retains 'ring the bull', an ancient pub game. It is played by swinging a ring attached to the ceiling by cord and attempting to hook it on to a bull's horn — or more often these days, a metal hook — on the wall some eight feet away. My own experience is that I manage to score around 1 hook in 500 whereas regulars achieve 18 or 19 hooks from 20 throws.

Other coaching houses on the main street included the Kings Head — which in 1807 advertised 'neat post chaise and able horses' — and the Old Queens Head where travellers on the Leeds to Skipton coaches were given bread and cheese as part of their fare. It was here in 1771 that a meeting of the jury was held to determine compensation for land required for the Leeds and Liverpool Canal. There were so many objectors that the meeting had to be adjourned to the Methodist Chapel. Other meetings held here included the first of the improvement commissioners — forerunners of the present day local government system — in 1847.

The Brown Cow, which has origins in the seventeenth century but has been rebuilt, was also a venue for official — and occasionally unofficial — meetings, for the local chartists made it their headquarters. In 1753 the Keighley and Bradford Turnpike Trust met here, and it also served as the petty sessions court. In an upstairs room was a private school run by Charles Hogg, who kept it in business after Forster's Education Act of 1870 which provided for universal schooling. The pub also had its own brewery, which closed before the Great War.

Meetings of the commissioners of the Leeds and Liverpool Canal were held during the late eighteenth century at the Elm Tree Inn, another coaching inn. (The improvement commissioners bought the pub in 1874 to enable them to widen the road.) In 1864 the Boars Head staged the town's first annual canary show. But despite this touch of graciousness, it was a pub that found little favour with the police, who reported unfavourably on it as a resort of dog fighters.

There are two pubs which recognise the powerful influence of two families in the area, the Ferrands Arms just off the main street and the wrongly spelled Busfeild Arms at nearby East Morton. The Ferrands is a insensitive, modern rebuild and is named after the family who lived on the St Ives estate for more than 300 years. An annex contained a hall for the Oddfellows Society until they built their own in 1862.

The incorrectly spelled Busfeild Arms at East Morton is mentioned in *Jane Eyre.*

For workers in the nearby towns, a visit to Dick Hudsons at High Eldwick was a Bank Holiday treat.

The Busfeild Arms, converted from three old cottages, was once known as the Hare and Hounds and is mentioned in Charlotte Brontë's novel *Jane Eyre*. Both the Busfield and the Ferrand families were involved in the public life of Bingley over many generations as magistrates, improvement commissioners and in other offices.

At High Eldwick is the best-loved pub in the area. Originally called the Fleece, it was known to millions as Dick Hudsons, which is now its official name. Richard Hudson was the licensee from 1850 to 1878, taking over from his father Tommy. It was a favourite day out spot for the mill workers of the West Riding towns, and was famous for its ham and eggs cooked in an eighteen inch frying pan. The pub also served roast beef and Yorkshire pudding for one shilling, and food was available from 6 am until 11 pm. Amongst the many famous visitors were the stage stars Vesta Tilley and Zena Dare and the Earl of Harewood.

It is another pub with literary connections — it can be found in Howard Spring's *Fame is the Spur*. Spring had visited there many times when working as a reporter on the *Yorkshire Observer* in Bradford. Whilst he enjoyed the atmosphere of the Fleece — in particular the ham and egg breakfasts which he and colleagues would consume before golfing at Hawksworth — it was the view which first attracted him:

'I sat on a boulder patterned with lichens, and the shadows thickened and far off the lights of the city came out upon the hills.'

During Queen Victoria's reign, John Ball lived in a small cottage near to the Fleece. He was known to all as 'Johnny Baker' because he baked hundreds of loaves in the inn's ovens. He also kept an illicit still and more than once was arrested, tried and fined. On one occasion the fine was a massive £50 which he paid at once in gold sovereigns. Johnny was a prize fighter and once fought all day with a giant Irishman until darkness forced a draw. Within the week they fought again and Johnny won.

THE CALDER VALLEY

'From Hull, Hell and Halifax, Good Lord deliver us.'

Yorkshireman's litany

Halifax has a wonderful history of inns, beerhouses, taverns and public houses, with one still in business which dates from the early days of the sixteenth century. Many others are of great antiquity, and have their origins in the latter part of that century and into the seventeenth. A survey taken in 1735 showed 22 licensed premises in the town, yet a century later 119 were recorded. (Wellington's Beerhouse Act was no doubt responsible for the rapid increase.) By 1897 the number had risen to 179.

The Union Cross in the old market is reckoned to be the oldest still in business. It was mentioned as early as 1535 but may have been earlier. Its name is unusual: the 'union' part probably relates to the marriage of Henry VII and Elizabeth of York which marked the union of the houses of Lancaster and York; and 'cross' almost certainly relates to its position opposite the market cross. At one time it was a centre for cockfighting.

The Old White Swan probably predated the Union Cross, being built around 1500 and rebuilt in 1858 when a formidable lady, Sarah Daxon, was the last landlady of the old pub and the first of the new. At the time of rebuilding an incident took place that is commemorated in verse:

> 'A great attraction in our good old town,
> Has been to see the Old White Swan pulled down.
> And hundreds have assembled every day,
> To see it taken bit by bit away...'

— and so on, to the tale of a man who was hit on the head by a ten pound stone dropped by a workman but who survived because he wore a hat he had bought from Wilsons of the Cornmarket. It must have been an early example of protective headgear!

Another Halifax building which dates from the middle of the eighteenth century is now the Bass House at Wards End. Inside what was once called Holly House has been built a new pub. The excellent listed building was originally built for the attorney, John Bentley, and later became a school dental surgery. In the cellar of the Ring o' Bells near the parish church there is a gravestone which dates from 1635; and the pub has a ghost called 'Wally' which causes things to disappear. Two ancient pubs — the Beehive and the Cross Keys in King Cross Street — were demolished in 1933 and one pub was built in their place, named with a singular lack of imagination the Beehive and Cross Keys, although the pub does display two fine mosaic signs.

Several Halifax pubs still in business have unusual names, including the Plummet Line in Bull Close Lane. This handsome hotel was built for the local brewery of Thomas Ramsden in 1898 and retains a splendid tiled nameplate. The name refers to a weighted line used by builders.

The Portman and Pickles in Market Street — formerly the Wheatsheaf — recognises the theatrical talents of two of the town's most famous sons, Eric Portman and Wilfred Pickles. Also in the central area can be found the Pot o' Four, named after a pot used by woolcombers to heat their combs.

The Running Man in Pellon Lane remembers those who attempted escape from the notorious Halifax gibbet, a form of guillotine. Escape could be made by running a certain distance — beyond the town's jurisdiction — but return brought back the vengeance of the gibbet. It gave rise to the Yorkshireman's litany:

'From Hull, Hell and Halifax, Good Lord deliver us.'

Hull was a place where only hard work with little reward came easily, and in Halifax you could be beheaded for stealing thirteen and a halfpence worth of cloth. Hell, it is claimed, could well be Elland. John Taylor, the water poet, was wont to quote it. He put into his own words the practice which ceased in 1650:

'At Halifax the law so sharpe doth deale,
The whoso more than thirteen pence doth steale,
They have a jyn that wondrous quick and well
Sends thieves all headless into heaven or hell.'

Theatrical, musical and literary traditions die hard in Halifax, not least in its inns and pubs. The Halifax Choral Society met at the Ovenden Cross Inn during the early nineteenth century, and rehearsals for the Halifax Philharmonic Society were held in the Kings Head in Cow Green when it was formed in the 1850's. In 1825, subscription concerts were held at the Pack Horse Inn in Southowram where the patrons were treated to '...works from German and Italian composers, followed by a Grand Ball'. Similar events were later held at the White Hall Inn at Hipperholme.

Daniel Defoe wrote much of the book more properly called *The Life and Strange Surprising Adventures of Robinson Crusoe, of York, Mariner, Written by Himself* at the Rose and Crown in Back Lane during his extensive travels through Britain. Edward Baines, the Leeds publisher, in his *Directory* of 1822 stated:

'The celebrated Daniel De Foe though not a native of Halifax, being obliged to abscond from his own neighbourhood on account of his political writings, came to this town, and enjoyed himself in writing — and in particular he is said to have composed here his famous romance of *Robinson Crusoe.*'

For centuries the Malt Shovel (which closed in 1913) was the venue for concerts and later for silent pictures. Discs were issued for two-pence which could be redeemed in the bar after the perfomances. Playbills issued in the 1750's referred to '...new theatre at the Talbot', and in 1762 to performances '...at the Theatre in the Old Cock yard'. Thirty years on the Halifax Harmonic Society was founded at the Old Cock.

But it was in 1854 when the Old Cock was to make its most indelible mark, not only in the history of the public house but in the commercial and economic annals of the world. Here in the Oak Room on the first floor was held the meeting to form the world's first building society

The Folly at Pye Nest is in the
shadow of another 'folly'.

— the Halifax. The room is retained with its elaborate carved
chimney piece and stained glass windows.

The temperance movement was strong in Halifax and the Calder
Valley — as one would expect from a bastion of Nonconformism. The
Band of Hope had several branches in the townships between Halifax
and Todmorden, often linked with the Methodist church. A British
Workmens Public House was opened in Gibbet Street which lasted
until 1877, when it was taken over by the Halifax Cocoa House
Company. Later it became the Railway Cocoa Tavern until it closed
in 1914.

Anyone travelling to the west of Halifax into the Calder Valley
cannot fail to see the 270 foot high Wainhouse Tower, a 'folly' which
in 1874 cost more than £10,000. It was built by John E Wainhouse
originally as a chimney connected by an underground flue to his
dyeworks in nearby Washer Lane. Later it may have been used as an
attempt by Wainhouse to upset his neighbour, Sir Henry Edwards,
the High Sherriff of the county, as it overlooked his house. Two years
later he built himself a new residence in the shadow of the chimney

in what has been described as the 'baroque gothick' style. This is now a public house appropriately named the Folly. One of the bars is called 'West Air', the original name of the house which is clearly displayed high on its frontage.

At nearby King Cross, in 1867 the seventeenth century Nags Head was being repaired and an old chimney was demolished. Behind it was found an orange banner with a blue border showing William of Orange on horseback and expounding 'To the glorious memory of 1688 and 1690'. These are the dates when the thirteen apprentice boys of Derry seized the keys of the city and slammed the gates in the faces of the troops of King James II, and of the Battle of the Boyne. Both events are celebrated by Orangemen to this day, but there is no

The Big Six takes its name from the brewing company once nearby.

obvious explanation as to why this banner should be found behind the chimney of a pub in the west end of Halifax.

The West End at Highroyd Well was purpose-built for the Richard Whitaker Brewery of Halifax by the local architects Petty and Ives in 1899, but the magistrates initially refused it a licence. For two years it was simply a refreshment house selling coffee, tea and soft drinks until the licence was granted in 1901. The Big Six, an excellent Victorian terraced pub, takes its unusual name from the hop ale and mineral water company that had its premises nearby. It was opened in the 1850's although the row of houses dates back before that. Its original name was the Bowling Green, but most people called it the Big Six so the name was changed around the turn of the century. The Halifax Chrysanthemum Society held its meetings there (one of its rules was that all blooms be displayed in Big Six bottles). Entry fees started at twopence and the top prize was a princely four shillings. In 1901 a satisfied local penned a fourteen verse paean to the pub:

> 'Teetotalers may rant and rave,
> But they can't help but say,
> That for decent jolly company,
> The Big Six leads the way.
>
> At this inn you'll ales find,
> There is no class distinction,
> Civility is always shown,
> What'er your lot or station.'

— and so on for another twelve verses.

Elland, although not as important a town as it once was, manages to retain a splendid sense of the past, with some narrow town centre streets and a delightful selection of inns and taverns. Slightly out of town on the north side of the River Calder are two pubs intrinsically linked with the transport history of the area. The Colliers on the Brighouse road has little to do with the men who hew coal, but more with the boats that carried it through the adjacent Elland lock. And

The Barge and Barrel in Elland dates from
the building of the nearby railway.

the Barge and Barrel, close to Elland bridge, stands opposite where
the town's railway station once was and dates from the building in the
1850's of the now closed line. It has recently been restored to its former
Victorian grandeur.

But Elland's most impressive and historic pub is the Fleece in
Westgate, which started life as a farmhouse in 1610. It has a stone
facade with four gables and some magnificent windows, with oak
abounding inside in its panelling, doors and fireplaces. It was here
that a terrible murder took place that is still remembered with an
inevitable ghost.

'Leathery Coit' — so called because of his hard, tanned skin — was
either a beggar or a traveller according to differing sources (the latter
tale is the most likely). He was brutally killed in an upstairs room at
the Fleece and his body dragged downstairs, leaving a trail of blood
which no amount of scrubbing would remove. For years, even today
perhaps, the Fleece was known as 'the inn with the bloody stairs'.
After this, reports followed that 'Leathery Coit' was seen driving his
carriage out of a nearby barn. A description of these events is framed
at the pub:

82

'Those who dared to watch might see an awful sight, for at midnight the doors of a large barn at the top of Westgate slowly opened without human agency, and there issued forth a travelling carriage with headless horses and headless coachman who drove furiously down Dog-lane to Old Earth, and thence returned. The coming of the spectral vision to have been usually accompanied by a sudden rush of wind, however quiet the night, and one can imagine how a sleeper, wakened suddenly by the violent gust or an unexpected noise, would listen, trembling, and say, ''There goes Leathery Coit''.'

Greetland had many more pubs at the turn of the century than it has now, and I am grateful to Peter Robinson in his paper *The Emergence of the Common Brewer in the Halifax District* for recalling a poem which names them all. It is called *A Hint to Drunkards*:

> 'How to begin our wondrous tale
> of those who sell this nasty ale.
> The first we view all in the stock
> is the beautiful Spring Rock.
>
> The next I think is the Sportsmans Inn
> where they do sell both ale and gin.
> If young or old to this place should go
> they are sure to find their deadliest foe.'

— and so on until the twelfth verse:

> 'So now to conclude and I hope their no ill
> if you call at Snowbelly's a pint he will fill.
> For many tried and are all turned adrift
> So I think we may venture to call it last shift.'

Barkisland has two very old inns: the Griffin dates from 1642 and the Fleece, which was once a farmhouse, from 1737. Also in the village, the New Rock Tavern is known as 't' 'ard end'.

GRIFFIN, BARKISLAND

P.W.R

The Griffin in Barkisland shows its age.

The Bridge in Ripponden stands next to the packhorse bridge over the River Ryburn, and can be established as one of the county's oldest establishments. It is thought to have been in business before 1313. Its magnificence prevails with a superb timber-framed interior. Amongst its patrons have been Daniel Defoe and King Christian of Denmark.

High above the main road is Soyland, with its cluster of interesting pubs. The Beehive, built in 1830, has its own welcoming rhyme:

> 'Within this hive we're all alive
> Good ale to make us funny.
> If you be dry, step in and try
> The flavour of our honey.'

The New Inn, built to serve the turnpike, has an attractive sundial that no longer works but which bears the Latin inscription:

> *'Ad hoc momento pandet aeternitas*
> *Latitude 53, 45 1764.'*

The Blue Ball, soaring above the other pubs in Soyland and on the packhorse route to Lancashire, commands some magnificent views. The pub dates from 1672 and is little changed. It also has the best tales to tell:

> 'The fortune teller's ball was blue
> A ghostly crystal awful hue
> A name on high for inns a few
> Where liquor food and horses new
> Could help the Roman chariots
> Through Blackstone Edge to Deva's View.'

It is haunted by a frightened ghost called Faith. She worked at the inn during the eighteenth century when the landlord was a tyrant known as Iron Ned. The place was a bolthole for highwaymen and footpads and Ned led a gang who roamed the countryside, raping, pillaging and robbing. He seduced Faith, and when she became pregnant decided to do away with her by drowning her on the moors.

Officially she was said to have committed sucicide — but most folk knew better. Faith's footsteps have been heard and sounds of struggle emit from the room that Iron Ned slept in.

In Rishworth the 200 year old Royal Hotel was formerly the council offices, and the Turnpike was the gatekeeper's lodge for the tollbar; the latter was once called the Derby Inn — with its official address as Derby Bar — and later a temperance hotel, and is said to be haunted.

The Yorkshire-Lancashire border was once straddled by the town of Todmorden, with its town hall cleaved by it. The river boundary flowed under the building and a sign still shows wool to the east and cotton to the west. The Rope and Anchor was built in 1787 and retains four distinct rooms — a lounge, a parlour, a tap room and a tiny snug. The Queen is an elegant Victorian railway hotel that was once linked by a private footbridge to the nearby station.

The uniquely-named Chesapeake and Shannon on the Halifax road dates from 1813. These were two ships in a naval battle outside Boston Harbour during the War of Independence. The American ship was captured by the Shannon and towed to Halifax in Nova Scotia, where it was eventually commissioned into the Royal Navy. At Lumbutts the Shepherds Rest is reputedly haunted; it dates from the fifteenth century and was a farmhouse for more than 300 years.

The White Lion in Hebden Bridge is one of the oldest buildings in the town. It was built in 1657 as a farm and developed as an inn when the turnpike opened 200 years ago. The Tythe Barn was converted from a sixteenth century barn, and was formally used as a tax office where the lord of the manor would collect his tythes in kind, usually as livestock or grain.

Cragg Vale owes its reputation to a gang, the 'Turvin Coiners', who used to clip around the edges of golden guineas, melt them down and make counterfeits. They were a wild bunch by all accounts. One of their haunts was the Dusty Miller in Mytholmroyd, and it was here in 1769 that two of them, Robert Thomas and Matthew Normanton, drank before going out to murder William Deighton, the Halifax excise officer. They were caught and tried, and hanged at York. During the nineteenth century the Dusty Miller was also used as a post office. The unfortunate Mr Deighton is remembered by a pub named after him in Halifax.

High on the northern side of the valley is Wadsworth, where 'on the great mount' is the Mount Skip — 'skip' meaning sheep. On the main valley road at Brearley is the Grove, behind which at one time was a small brewery. The pub was the 'tap' of Harvey and Company who brewed from 1863 to 1920, although they were taken over by Richard Whitaker and Company of Halifax along with twenty pubs in 1905.

Moving eastwards, in Luddenden Foot is the currently-named Coach and Horses. It started life in 1877 as the General Rawdon, named after General Sir George Rawdon who helped restore Charles II to the throne in 1660. Up the hill in Luddenden can be found the Lord Nelson, built originally as a house in 1634. It became an inn called the White Swan in 1745, and took its present name in 1805 after the admiral's victory at Trafalgar. Branwell Brontë was a regular here whilst he worked at the local railway station.

Across the valley near Sowerby is the Travellers Rest, a former farmhouse which dates from 1649, and in the village is the Church Stile, next to the parish church and used in former times — and no doubt today — to refresh parishioners travelling from outlying areas.

The Triangle gave its name to the village it now stands in. It was established as a packhorse inn in 1767 on a triangular piece of land. It now belongs to the Bass Brewery, whose red triangle trade mark was ready-made for the sign.

The oldest pub in Sowerby Bridge is probably the Puzzle Hall Inn, enigmatic in its name and architectural styles. It retains a tower that once housed a brewery to produce a local stout, although this building is much newer than the rest of the pub. The brewery was built towards the end of the last century to cater for the pub alone. In 1912 one of its owners, John Platt, fell to his death from the roof of the pub whilst carrying out repairs. It ceased to brew in 1936 when it was acquired by Wards Brewery of Sheffield.

The Ash Tree Restaurant was formerly known as the Wharf Hotel and my father, Alex Pepper, was the licensee here in the 1950's. (He pointed out to me the different spelling of the pub's name — 'Wharf' on the sign and 'Wharfe' on the licence plate above the door — and it was this that started my interest in the public house.) The present building was only a pub from 1922, its business being transferred from across the road when the original was declared unfit. (This was an unusual decision on the part of the magistrates at that time, who were usually only too anxious to close pubs down.) The original pub was in Cawsey House, named because it stood on the causeway or packhorse route between Manchester and Leeds. It became a pub in 1747 called the Mermaid, changing to the Wharf in 1898. The original building had a large assembly room, and the present one used to have an attractive central well and gallery.

In 1912 the first motor buses to run out of Halifax had their terminus at the New Inn at Mount Tabor. It was the brewery tap for Aspinall's Brewery, which stopped brewing in 1932. The nearby Stone Chair began life as a beerhouse for workers at the stone quarries in the district. And the Delvers at Wainstalls was recently renamed to recognise the once-thriving quarrying industry.

Much of the oak panelling in the Cat i' th' Well near Wainstalls came from the now demolished folly of Castle Carr. The pub is situated in the valley of the Catywell Brook from where it takes its name. It was built around 1700 and, in the late nineteenth century, was the home of John Preston, a well-known lay preacher and eccentric.

There is a New Delight at Wainstalls, one of four of that name to have existed in Calderdale. The name is almost certainly taken from Milton's *Paradise Lost*: 'Heav'n's last best gift, my ever new delight.' This was once called the Travellers Rest. Originally it was on the packhorse route from Halifax to Haworth, and was also the terminus for tramcars between 1906 and 1908. The pub has a ghost which lives in the cellar and mischievously turns the lights on and off.

The first friendly society or 'sick club' in the Halifax area was founded at the Illingworth Cross Inn in 1788. It was known as the Ovenden Brotherly Society. Subscriptions of two shillings each quarter were paid at meetings held at the inn, and each member was expected to spend at least threepence during the meeting. Sick pay was five shillings and sixpence a week, with a death benefit of five pounds, also payable on the death of a wife. The society later bought a plot of land and for £600 built six cottages, known as 'club cottages', which now stand in Club Lane. The society later moved to the White Lion.

The Crown and Anchor at Mixenden pays tribute to a former landlord with its 'Doc Shire' lounge. The Halifax brewery of Richard Whitaker and Company had a range of beer called 'Shire' ales and Herbert Seston, a portly Mr Pickwick character, was the model for their advertisements.

High on the hilltop at Ploughcroft is the Sportsman Inn. It was built before 1770 and was originally a farmhouse. The sporting connections are continuous. In its early days as an inn it provided stabling for huntsmen and later had its own cricket ground. Today it has a squash court and an all-weather ski slope.

It was once a venue for knurr and spell, sometimes known as 'working men's golf'. It is played with a stick or club and the objective is to strike a projectile as far as possible. Distances are measured in scores (twenty yards). It had a renaissance in recent years at the Spring Rock in Barkisland. Nipsy is a similar game played mainly in the Barnsley area and another of the genre, billets, can be found in pubs in the upper Calder Valley. Another favourite game of the moorland pubs was 'twarlin'' or twirling. A bucket of beer with a rope attached to the handle would be swung around by the player to see who could reach the widest circle. Its popularity seems to have waned — I suppose that is understandable, although some more exotic pub games have appeared on the scene.

It is claimed that there were only ever five windmills in the Halifax area, and one of them at Northowram gave its name both to the Windmill Tavern and the Windmill Hill Brewery. The mill itself was demolished in 1854 so the pub obviously predates this, but the brewery only operated from 1899 and closed in 1908. The Old White Beare in Norwood Green claims to date from 1533 although the name comes from a ship that fought against the Armada. It had its own brewery and the equipment has been preserved in the Shibden Hall Folk Museum on the outskirts of Halifax.

Tucked away in the narrow upper Shibden Valley to the north of the main road into Halifax can be found the Shibden Mill Inn. It was built in 1649 for the workers at the former water-powered corn mill from which it took its name. The Lister family lived for many years at Shibden Hall, and their coat of arms can be found above the door of the Stump Cross Inn, which used to be part of the estate.

In Brighouse the George Hotel once had its own brewery. This important coaching house was built in 1815 by a Doctor Day and substantially altered in 1890. As its coaching function receded the owners encouraged its use as a waiting house for railway passengers, it being just a five minute walk from the station. The brewery operated from 1878 to 1912 and James Dyson was the owner for around twenty years of that time. ('Dysons Pure Bitter' is still advertised but no longer sold.) It had an important social function too, being the headquarters of both Brighouse Cycling Club and Brighouse Football Club — 'the Rangers'.

The oldest licensed house in Raistrick is the Star. It was built in the early nineteenth century, and for many years was the only inn in the district where a newspaper was available to the public. Each morning queues of thirty to forty people waited to read it and presumably refresh themselves as well. The Globe is an unassuming Victorian building where one would expect little exciting to happen. But in 1910 the landlord hanged himself and his wife, rather than disturb the settled nature of the pub, continued serving until the session was over and then called in the police.

COLNE, HOLME AND SPEN

'..I know no part of the West Riding where the sterling qualities of a moorland race have been better preserved.'

J H Snowden

High on the Pennine slopes are a clutch of pubs known to walkers over the decades and to motorists in more recent times. They have served as direction posts, rescue houses and, more simply, good places to be. Some are long gone: Bill O' Jacks on the Marsden to Manchester road, pulled down to allow a reservoir to be built, was one; it was four miles on from the Isle of Skye, 1,600 feet up on Wessenden Head and now giving its name to the road that crosses into Lancashire. But perhaps most famous of all, Nont Sarahs at Scammonden, is still with us. It was named after Aunt Sara, the landlady in the middle of the nineteenth century.

Another of this cluster of inns that rest more than 1,000 feet above sea level is the Floating Light on the road over Standedge. It derived its name from the illusion created in misty weather that the pub lights were floating. When it was rebuilt fifty years ago there was no electricity, so two large oil lamps were used to illuminate the building and which remain there to this day.

The moors drop west here into a pocket of the old West Riding that is lost these days to the strange-sounding county of Greater Manchester. Hugging the hillside as it falls towards Denshaw is the Rams Head, more affectionately known as 't' Owd Tupps'. This seventeenth century inn is isolated and often cut off by bad weather in winter. Little has changed here, with wooden settles, open fires in all rooms, and casks of ale on stillages behind the bar with service from stainless steel jugs. It could easily be many person's ideal place to be cut off in! And the views are magnificent.

Lower down is the Junction, an eighteenth century former coaching inn with thick stone walls and open fires, and the Black Horse, a mid nineteenth century stone-built pub now well below the line of the present road. On the old road there was a ford here, and pubs were often situated near to such passing places. In nearby Diggle, the Diggle Hotel is to be found near to the entrance to Standedge Tunnel on the Huddersfield Narrow Canal. The tunnel is more than three miles long and more than 600 feet above sea level. It was in this pub that meetings of the Huddersfield Canal Society were held to agree to its construction.

The Swan Inn in Dobcross dates from 1765 and was formerly called the Kings Arms, of which there is a pleasant memory in the form of a delightful etched glass door. It is a grade two listed building. One family has provided the landlord for the Horse and Jockey in Dobcross since it was rebuilt in 1920, and in Lydgate the White Hart is another listed building which was first licensed in 1789. The eighteenth century Farrars Arms at Glasscroft retains its original beams and room layout; the lord of the manor — Farrar of Shaw Mere — collected taxes here from his tenants.

The Cross Keys in Uppermill is an eighteenth century stone-built listed building that overlooks Saddleworth Church. The public bar is known as Buckley's Kitchen, recalling a rather ageing former curate with lodgings at the inn who, one night in a drunken stupor, attacked a woman with a red hot poker and burnt out one of her eyes. The 'kitchen' retains a Yorkshire range. It is one of several pubs in the former Saddleworth Urban District Council area that are tied to the John Willy Lees Brewery of Middleton Junction in Lancashire.

The Sair Inn can be found at the top of a steep lane off the main Manchester to Huddersfield road at Linthwaite. Today it has the distinction of being the area's only home brew pub, but historically it is the name that attracts most attention. Until recently it was yet another New Inn, but had been long known locally in the Colne Valley dialect as 't' Saah'. Various interpretations have been given for this. The contented sow on the modern sign is one, and a response of 'saar' or 'sour' to a potential customer's query as to 'what's the ale like?' is another. But the most likely is that it followed an early owner of the pub known to all as 'John o' t' Saah'. John lived next to an open stream and 'saah' — or more properly 'sough' — means a rushing sound.

When 'John o' t' Saah' moved to the New Inn, the name moved with him and became attached to the pub. In 1876 when Eli Dyson took over at the New Inn he became 'Eli o' t' Saah', the name passing on like an inherited title. He is the pub's best-remembered landlord and held the licence well into the twentieth century. In 1984 the present landlord, Ron Crabtree, renamed the pub and gave it what some experts believe to be a wrongly spelled title, 'Sair'. Nonetheless it provides a talking point for what remains an excellent and unspoilt example of an eighteenth century inn, with many rooms and stone-flagged floors. To recognise his illustrious predecessor, Mr Crabtree brews and sells a formidable ale called 'Old Eli'.

At Slaithwaite — or 'Slough 'it' as the locals call it — a pub officially called the White House takes its nickname 'Alcanders' after a former landlord, one Alexander Holdroyd. He held court here in the mid-nineteenth century and was something of a character. Local records describe him as an 'agricultural engineer and inventor'. Amongst several — usually unsuccessful — inventions, he attempted like many others to fly like a bird. He donned home-made wings and launched himself off the roof of the pub — only to land in the muck midden!

Wills O' Nats at Meltham is another pub — of which Yorkshire spawns many — which are known officially by one name but to the locals by another. William Dyson had been the popular landlord of the New Inn in the 1880's, and the name came about because he, 'Will', was the son of Nathaniel, 'Nat'. However, it remained the New Inn until 1975 when public demand occasioned the change. It was also a farmhouse, a popular place where travellers on horseback were made welcome and fed and watered.

In the eighteenth century, Vicars of Huddersfield were also publicans, and the Rose and Crown stood where the vicarage once was. Chaises were hired out from here — as they were from the Pack Horse in Kirkgate. The Pack Horse was rebuilt in 1778 by Sir John Ramsden, a man who made a decisive impact on Huddersfield lasting even to this day, with the Huddersfield Broad Canal and several streets and buildings named after him. (The Ramsdens were Lords of the Manor of Huddersfield for many years.) Sir John spent £520 to refurbish the Pack Horse and the rent of £117 for the inn, stables, yards and crofts was regarded as very high, although it was considered one of the most imposing buildings in the town. Also in Kirkgate was the Swan, later renamed the White Swan to avoid confusion with the nearby Swan with Two Necks.

There were several pubs in the market place, including the Brown Cow which employed its own bellman; 'Cockle Jack' came from Leeds and used his vocal capacity to tell the burghers of Huddersfield about 'Cockles and mussels sold in the Brown Cow at fourpence a quart'. The White Boar doubled up as a butcher's shop and it was here that an early instance of short measure was recorded. John Walker was the landlord in 1734 and the manor court fined him five shillings for several cases of short measure in ale.

Next to the Brown Cow in the south-west corner of the market place were the Kings Arms, with its own brewhouse, and the Horse and Jockey; and on the northern side, the Queens Head, which faced out of the square with shops linking it from a courtyard. It had stables and was described as 'impressive' by contemporary sources. But the most outstanding of the buildings in the market place and certainly the most historic inn in Huddersfield is the George Hotel.

It started life as the George Inn shortly after George I came to the throne in 1714, a consequence of substantial developments in the market place. It was not only a coaching inn but a 'chaise house' as well, providing a taxi service for richer customers. In 1800 its rent was £315 — described as 'massive' — but this did include a number of merchant's shops behind the inn. The George provided the town's council chamber in early days, and was the venue for meetings of the turnpike trustees. In 1850 it was 're-erected' rather than rebuilt.

But the real claim to historical fame for the George Hotel — as it was by then — came in 1895, when a historic meeting was held there at which the forerunner of the present Rugby Football League was formed. The whole of the early history of this sport appears to have been linked with public houses. What were originally rugby union clubs were often founded in inns, pubs and hotels. The Little Saddle Inn in Dewsbury saw the formation of that town's club in 1876. Its landlord, William Blackburn, lent £15 to the Dewsbury Athletic and Football Club and then paid out another half guinea to become its first patron. Halifax had their headquarters at the Upper George Hotel, and when they won the Yorkshire Challenge Cup in 1894, 't' Owd Tin Pot' was paraded through the streets of the town headed by a brass band.

The breakaway from Rugby Union came about over the issue of 'broken time' payments to players who had to miss work to play in matches. It was a classic early case of the North-South divide. The wealthy clubs of the south attracted players to whom time off from work was of no consequence, but in the North — Lancashire and Yorkshire in particular — many of the players were artisans to whom a full pay packet was vitally important. The issue came to a head in the 1890's and many meetings were held — some in secret — in the pubs of the great cities: the West Riding Hotel and the Mitre in Leeds; the Alexandra and the Talbot in Bradford; and the Spread Eagle in Manchester.

In December 1894 a secret meeting in the George Hotel in Huddersfield was the first of a series that culminated with the historic one on the 29th August 1895 that is commemorated there today by a plaque:

'The clubs here represented decided to form a Northern Rugby Football Union, and pledge themselves to push forward without delay its establishment on the principle of payment for bona-fide broken time only.'

And push forward without delay they did, by electing a committee which met on the 3rd September to arrange a full list of matches to be played four days later.

John Hanson, a historian of note, found several anecdotes relating to the pubs of Huddersfield. He wrote of men found guilty of petty larceny being flogged through the streets of the town from the Cloth Hall to the Dog Inn. And he recorded that the White Lion in Cross Church Street was the first inn in Huddersfield to have gas lighting.

It came in 1878 when Mr Waite, a plumber, filled a leather bag with gas and used bellows and an attached pipe through a hole in a table. It was lit '…to the great astonishment of the jovial, tho' not specially intelligent frequenters of the house'. Almost a hundred years later the White Lion was the birthplace of the Kirklees branch of the Campaign for Real Ale.

Suburban Huddersfield is full of surprises. A pub at Lindley Moor is called the Wappy Springs after a former brewery on the site; and the Slubbers Arms on the Halifax road takes its name from a worker in the textile trade. The Fly Boat was once a bargee's pub, and the Crimea on Primrose Hill dates from 1793, although its present name must date from sixty years or so later. In Lindley the Black Bull — with its original wooden bar — is a listed building in which the present gents' toilets were once a grocer's shop.

Above the town, at Almondbury on Castle Hill, there is evidence of a fort dating from the third century BC and of later occupation by the Romans. The first licensed property here was built in 1830 as a private house with its own gooseberry garden. Soft drinks such as ginger beer were sold there, and gooseberries could be purchased at fourpence a quart. Later it was licensed and then replaced by the Castle Hill Hotel, built in 1852 next to a tower which celebrates Queen Victoria's jubilee, and which many people assume to have given the hill its name.

Church and inn stand well together as twin pillars of communities. There are good examples all over the county, none better than at Kirkheaton where the Beaumont Arms is known locally as 'Kirksteel' or 'Kirkstile'. The Beaumont family owned much of the land in the immediate area, and several of them are recognised in the adjacent St John's Church which, although Victorian, has a much older status. The pub is an interesting collection of buildings, and was at one time a court house with the long chamber preserved on the first floor. Below the pub is a cell and a passage to the church. (The site is mentioned in the *Domesday Book.*) An arch links the stables to the road and through it a former landlord drove his horse-drawn hearse, in the tradition of former times when they combined the job of innkeeper with another

The Beaumont Arms at Kirkheaton was once an undertakers.

The medieval nuns of nearby Kirklees Priory brewed their own ale at the
Three Nuns in Mirfield.

profession — in this case that of an undertaker!

The present day mock-Tudor facade of the Three Nuns at Mirfield hides the inner original shell of a medieval inn where nuns once brewed their own ale. It was linked with the nearby twelfth century Kirklees Priory, where there was a malthouse. The priory adds another piece into the amazing jigsaw of the tale of Robin Hood in Yorkshire, for it is here that his grave is supposed to be.

The 300 year old Gray Ox at Hartshead has retained the unusual — though not incorrect — spelling ever since a signwriter made what was thought to be an error, but one which appealed to the owner at that time. At Hartshead Moor the Old Pack Horse and the New Pack Horse stand opposite one another; both were once coaching houses.

The Saville Arms at Hunsworth was built in 1601 as a farmhouse, and had lights to guide travellers over the moors. It was extended in the eighteenth century when it became an inn. The eighteenth century Albion at Liversedge has the ghost of a 'lady in silk' — perhaps yet another 'grey lady' — who walks the corridors of a pub in which she is supposed to have been stabbed to death.

The Saville Arms at Hunsworth has mullioned windows and recesses where lights were once placed to guide travellers over the moors.

The Shears Inn at Hightown almost certainly takes its name from the heavy shears used by croppers in the woollen cloth industry during the eighteenth and early ninetenth centuries. It was here that the Luddites of the Spen Valley met with colleagues from Huddersfield to plan their subversive operations against their employers for introducing machinery that would make their jobs redundant. (They took their name from a young halfwit called Ned Ludd from Leicestershire who smashed some stocking frames in 1790 and achieved lasting notoriety.) In February 1812 the disaffected workers attacked a wagonload of machinery bound for William Cartwright's mill in Rawfolds. Two months later 150 Luddites attacked the mill itself, but found Cartwright waiting for them; a fierce gun fight took place in which two of the attackers were badly wounded. They were taken to the Star Inn at Roberttown where they died. The militia were called in, but found the locals in sympathy with the croppers and none were arrested.

There was horse racing at Roberttown in the early nineteenth century on common land known as Peep Green. George Humble, the landlord of the Globe at Millbridge, was the patron and he worked hard to attract professional jockeys to the races. Later, after a jockey was killed in a race that crossed the Leeds to Huddersfield turnpike, they lost their glitter and eventually it became simply a pleasure fair.

Church Steps seems popular as a pub name in the Heavy Woollen district, with the best-known one at Batley. This was originally called the Fleece, and was built for worshippers at the nearby parish church who had travelled from as far afield as Morley and Gildersome. An underground passage is said to link the inn and the church. It was a popular meeting place for local organisations — the churchwardens used it — and later it became Batley's first town hall. The Black Bull was also used for meetings and the first masons' lodge in the town was formed there.

Businessmen used the Bull and Butcher, which was built in 1723. The yard was the venue for fairs but it was closed in 1900 after a report of the police to the magistrates that it was '...a house of ill-repute, a haunt of thieves and prostitutes...'

Fairs and theatrical performances by travelling players were held in the late nineteenth century on a roundabout opposite the Talbot Hotel. It was built in 1870 by William Talbot and was not — unlike many others of the same title — named after the hunting dog. The George also had theatrical connections, with the stars of the local theatre staying there.

The Wilton takes its name from the family name of the Earls of Edgerton who owned much land in the district. It had a ghost called 'Oscar' who would turn off the beer pumps during his mischievous periods. It was another pub used by public bodies — the local board of health met there. The Wilton Arms and Bridge was renamed in 1823 after a bridge was built over the adjacent beck.

The Knottingley Wells takes its name from a nearby well used for watering horses, although the present building only dates from around 1930. The Havercroft had two main rooms and what was known as a 'stand-up'. It was a tiny room with access to the bar but with room for only two people to stand up in. The Commercial Arms, once called the Old House at Home, had clog dancing every Saturday night as part of its attractions. One landlord in late Victorian days was Ben Chappell, a well-known local cricketer. He played for Batley Cricket Club in a match against an eleven raised by the famous doctor, W G Grace. Chappell bowled him out for a duck. The doctor was not best pleased, turning to the local hero and exploding: 'They [the crowd] came to see me bat, not you bowl!'

Another similarly-named pub, the Commercial Inn in Clerk Green, was once kept by a widow, Grace Redfearn, who had twenty-one children. She had a slate in the bar on which she chalked the customers' names and the amount they owed. She asked one man to 'wipe his slate clean' — and he did just that with a wet cloth, thus clearing off the records of all the debtors.

There was an active temperance movement in Batley from around 1830. Predominant in it was Richard Gragon, who obtained 3,000 pledges against drink from customers in his shop. Another was Joseph Auty, a local councillor who used his position to secure the closure of beerhouses. He was a famous orator and made an annual speech in the town on temperance which often drew attendances of thousands. In the 1870's a number of coffee houses were built but — as elsewhere in the West Riding — they were shortlived, none remaining as proponents of temperance into the twentieth century.

The use of public houses as courtrooms was common in the area. The Black Bull in Birstall (a listed building) was used as such until 1839. The first floor room where the last trial was held has remained laid out unaltered ever since. The Horse and Jockey is said to be the second oldest building in Birstall. The Coach and Six — a rare name in a category that has spawned many pubs — was rebuilt on the site of a former coaching inn on the Leeds to Huddersfield road; and the Old Wine and Spirit Vaults close by was a former wine warehouse.

The oldest pub in Dewsbury is the Woodman which probably originates from the early seventeenth century — although a number of others come close. The Saville Arms on Church Street is said to have connections with the Civil War, but probably dates from 1767 when nearby All Saints Parish Church was rebuilt. It is another pub known as the 'Church Steps', and actually has its car park in part of the church grounds. It is thought to be the only pub in Britain that is built on consecrated ground.

The enigmatic architecture of the Market House in the centre of Dewsbury.

Dewsbury's Royal Hotel in Northgate was the venue for a meeting in 1876 where the plans were laid for the town's first infirmary. It was also the home of what became known as the 'Royal Hotel Liberals', a clique of politicians that controlled the town council in the late nineteenth century. An earlier Royal Hotel had stood in the market place; this was the scene of Poor Law riots during 1837 whilst it had been home to the magistrates' court. The Market House is a turn-of-the-century pub with some interesting and varied architectural styles. The tap room has an unusual if not unique set of five handpumps.

Across the moors and close to the Derbyshire border, in the moorland village of Holme, the Fleece Inn has been written into song by the Holme Valley Beadlers, who met there at one time:

> 'On a fine hunting morn,
> With his hounds and his horn,
> Charles Brook and his beadles,
> Came hunting to Holme.
> And at the Fleece Inn,
> The hunt did begin,
> All brave and honest sportsmen,
> Did aloo and sing.
> Here's a health to all hunters from city and town,
> Likewise the best sportsmen that's round about Holme.'

Holmfirth is well-known as the home of the Balmforth comic postcard firm, so it is not surprising to find a pub there called the Postcard displaying one of the more popular designs on its sign.

But not so well-known is the fact that comic films were made in the town before the turn of the century. One of the characters who acted in them was Fred Beaumont, known as 'Shiner' because he was a french polisher. Once he was polishing up a couple of coffins in the tap room of the Jolly Hatter when he heard a customer arriving. His nature being such, he hid in one of the coffins and, after the fellow got his drink and the landlord repaired to the other bar, he raised the lid and called out: 'Aw I am cowd, Aw I am cowd'. The customer — who had already had a few — dashed out to the next pub and told the assembled drinkers: 'At Jolly Hatters they're burying t' buggers wick [alive] there!'

Historic connections spread far and wide through Yorkshire's pubs, almost like questions in a history examination. For example: 'Connect the Stanhope Arms at Dunford Bridge with two pubs at Horsforth to the north of Leeds.' The simple answer is that the names of the two pubs are also the Stanhope Arms, but the more complex answer lies in the fact that the pub on the Derbyshire border was once the hunting lodge of the Spencer Stanhope family of Cannon Hall at Cawthorne near Barnsley. The Spencers had lived at Cannon Hall since the 1660's, but when John Spencer died in 1775 the line became extinct. His eldest sister Ann married Walter Stanhope of Horsforth and their son Walter — heir to John Spencer — took the name Walter Spencer Stanhope in his uncle's memory. It was Walter who built the hunting lodge which later became a public house. There are also Spencer Arms at Cawthorne and Barugh Green.

High on the moors towards Penistone, the Flouch Inn has been a haven for many years for travellers cut off by the snows. But it begs the question; why such a name? It opened in 1827 as the New Inn but from there on the story takes two directions. One says that it is named after a former landlord who had a speech impediment — a 'slouch lip'; and the other claims that it was to have been renamed the Plough and — either whilst being erected or during a storm — parts of the letters P and G fell off.

SOUTH YORKSHIRE

'A town the size of Sheffield, having so many breweries, required a proportionate number of outlets, and it had them in plenty.'

Roy Davey

The steel city of Sheffield has many public houses with fascinating histories, and can point to more communal remembrances about them than anywhere else in Yorkshire. The flood of 1864, the mobsters of the 1920's and the blitz of 1940 — all have left a significant mark on the drinking habits and habitats of its population.

It is a city, too, which spawned many breweries, and during the latter years of the nineteenth century there were more than thirty common brewers there. It was about this time that the number of licensed establishments reached its peak: 560 inns and hotels were registered in 1883, along with 682 beerhouses with an 'on' licence; and to add to this there were well over 600 'off' licences, often corner shops where beer could only be sold to take away. The 'beer only' pubs have almost vanished, and in 1981 the total number of public houses in the city had droppped to 666, which is still 50 more than Leeds despite a smaller population.

The industrial base of Sheffield led to many beerhouses being built close to the steel mills and the heavy engineering factories. It was thirsty work and those thirsts needed quenching. Roy Davey, in his highly entertaining booklet *Pubs and People Around Sheffield,* writes:

'...it was common to see the "odd lad" in the mill or forge on his way to or from the public house carrying a broomstick, suspended from which there would be perhaps a dozen enamelled cans with bent wire handles. Several trips might be made during the course of a shift to fetch beer for the set for whom he worked.'

The Cross Keys in Handsworth is claimed as the oldest inhabited building in Sheffield mainly, one suspects, because one of the timbers in the bar has been dated as twelfth century. It stands in the corner of St Mary's churchyard, and from its cellar is a tunnel leading to the

THE  HOTEL,

ANGEL STREET,
SHEFFIELD.

FREDERIC WILKINSON, Proprietor.

Commercial, Family & Posting House.
HOT AND COLD BATHS.

This Hotel is in the most central part of the Town.

ANGEL INN LIVERY & BAIT STABLES,
ANGEL STREET, SHEFFIELD.

GEORGE MITCHELL,
LICENSED TO LET
POST HORSES, WEDDING AND PARTY CARRIAGES,
HANSOM'S PATENT & OTHER CABS,
OMNIBUSES FOR PLEASURE EXCURSIONS,
HEARSES,
MOURNING COACHES, AND FAMILY FUNERAL OMNIBUSES.

The Angel was one of the earliest coaching inns, and survived the coming of the railways.

manor house. (This has now been blocked off.) The Old Queens Head in Pond Hill is said by Nicholas Pevsner in his *Buildings of England* to be the oldest house in inner Sheffield. On its construction in the late fifteenth or early sixteenth century it was referred to as a 'hawle in the ponds'. It was used for a period as a laundry for Sheffield Castle and, during refurbishment in 1949, the owners John Smith of Tadcaster discovered some timbers that were possibly original.

The Carbrook Hall Hotel on Attercliffe Common dates from 1623, but the original building on the site was constructed in 1176. The present house was built by Thomas Bright and is listed as of historic and architectural interest. It has a Jacobean oak fireplace, panelling by Leonard Gill and a fine period kitchen. Despite all this it was once described as a 'common beerhouse'.

According to the CAMRA guide *Real Beer in South Yorkshire,* the Britannia in Attercliffe is the third oldest pub in Sheffield. Although it bears a date of 1772 on a gable it is thought to be older. It was originally two houses belonging to Benjamin Huntsman, a steel magnate and the inventor of crucible steel (possibly the only invention to have a theatre named after it!). In its time it became a workshop, then a school, later a shop and then a public house. Just to complicate matters even further, the White Swan at Greenhill claims to be more than 300 years old. It retains many rooms, one of which has a stone cast of Wolsey's head.

Sheffield had many coaching inns, but the best known are no longer with us. The Tontine died as a result of the railway reaching the town, and the Angel Inn was a casualty of a German bomb in 1940. The Angel was built in the early eighteenth century and Angel Street remains named after the inn. It was one of the early coaching inns, and in 1760 the landlord, Sam Glanville, sent the first coach to London. There was great rivalry and speed was of the essence. By 1788 the Angel coach took 29 hours to reach London and by 1825, 22 hours.

In 1836 a local diarist recorded that '...170 gents dined at the Cutlers' Hall to an excellent dinner by Mr Hancock of the Angel Inn'. The Angel survived the coming of the railway and in 1862, the landlord, George Mitchell, advertised that he was:

'Licensed to let post horses, wedding and party carriages, Hansom's patent and other cabs, Omnibuses for pleasure excursions, Hearses, Mourning coaches and family funeral omnibuses, Livery and Bait stables.'

In December 1940 the Angel was completely destroyed by a German bomb during one of the two massive air raids on the city.

The Tontine had a greater reputation than the Angel. Its origins arose from the demand by the Sheffield gentry for a suitable building in which to hold meetings and fashionable functions. Fifty leading citizens each subscribed £100 to a 'tontine' to provide the capital for the inn to be built. The system worked in such a way that profits were shared annually while the shareholders remained alive, but eventually there would be a single owner. It was a gamble on who lived longest!

The pub opened in 1785 and was a very smart affair, much more lavish than any other house in the town. There was a sixty foot long dining room and a myriad of smaller rooms available for private functions. Accomodation was available for guests and their servants, and there was stabling for sixty horses. In its heyday thirteen coaches a day were leaving for London, with other services connecting with Birmingham, Leeds and Carlisle. The Tontine was noted for smartness and efficiency and provided exactly what its owners desired.

As a meeting place, however, there is an ugly scar in its history. At an election meeting in 1832, stones were thrown, one of which struck a magistrate. He sent to Rotherham for the troops. and when they arrived he ordered them to open fire on the mob. The usual practice was to fire a round of blanks, but for some reason this did not happen; three men and a boy were killed and another man died later from his wounds. A coroner's inquest returned a verdict of 'justifiable homicide'. In 1850, with the coming of the steam age, the building was pulled down and a market hall erected on the site.

Yet another part of the Robin Hood legend can be found in the area, with a pub named after the outlaw-cum-hero at Little Matlock in Stannington. The area takes its name from the spa town of Matlock in Derbyshire, and the pub was built on the site of a spa development by the Reverend Thomas Halliday in 1794 that failed. Loxley Chase is nearby and this is supposed to be the birthplace of Robin of Locksley. Robin Hood's Well can be found in neighbouring woods.

The Duncan Gilmour Brewery spawned some excellent houses in its time — none better than the White Lion in Heeley. It has some fine etched glass windows, with an interesting reversed 'N' in the spelling of 'Windsor Ales'. There are five unusually-named rooms, including a 'Private Smoke Room' and a 'Bagatelle Room'. The 'Priest's Hole' connects the bar parlour to a back servery but this has no religious connections; it is merely a short cut to serve drinks to an otherwise isolated room.

Another fine Gilmour pub, although of more recent build, is the Pheasant on Attercliffe Common. The present house dates from only 1927 but its origins lay in the seventeenth century. For many years it was run by two families, the Howdens and the Fowlers, both of whom were involved in the trades of scissor-making and cutlers. The pub's

The White Lion in Heeley — note the spelling of 'Windsor'.

name comes from the gamelands that surrounded it 300 years ago, and sporting connections have followed through the years. At the turn of the century there was a large sports field attached to the pub. Professional sprint races were held there, with heavy betting going on. The present building houses a snooker room — a rarity these days — with splendid tiered seating.

There was bareknuckle boxing, too, at the Pheasant, and the Great Bendigo, otherwise known as William Thompson, fought both there and at the Sportsmans Group in Penistone Road. He was one of triplets known as Shadrac, Meshac and Abendigo who were born in 1811 in Nottingham. He became heavyweight champion in 1832, and one of his fights lasted ninety-eight rounds. He was also a roughneck and spent twenty-eight terms in jail for various offences. When he moved to Sheffield he must have left his bad ways behind, for he became landlord of the Manchester Hotel in Nursery Street. His fame was such that a town in Australia is named after him.

Despite the fact that the nearest course to the city is twenty miles away at Doncaster, there have been at least four pubs in the area named after winning racehorses. The Beeswing Tavern in Hartshead was named after a most successful flat racer that won the Doncaster Cup four times, including three times in succession from 1840 to 1842. (There are similarly-named pubs at York and at East Cowton in the North Riding.) Two Derby winners are celebrated by the Cossack in Howard Street, which won the 1847 race at odds of five to one, and the Cremorne in London Road which took the title in 1872. The Why Not in Burngreave won the premier steeplechase, the Grand National, in 1894. And in Fargate a pub named Well Run Dimple is thought to relate to the success of yet another horse.

There are many other pubs in the city with sporting histories. The Adelphi, on the site of where the Crucible Theatre now is, can claim a double achievement: it was here in 1863 that the Yorkshire County Cricket Club was formed, to be followed four years later by the Sheffield Wednesday Association Football Club. The Cricket Inn — in what is now Hyde Park — had its own ground from 1826, and in 1833 a Yorkshire side played a Norfolk team there. The ground

The nineteenth century Victoria Park Hotel.

later became a greyhound stadium. The Rose and Crown at Darnall was rebuilt at the turn of the century and proudly proclaims itself as the headquarters of the British Whippet Racing Association.

Pigeon racing is a popular sport in Sheffield, and many pubs have their own clubs. At one time fanciers used bacon boxes — large containers used to import bacon from the continent — as lofts or huts. A pub called the Marshall Tavern in Pitsmoor Road was so small that it was nicknamed 'the Bacon Box'. And to show that not all is new, particularly in the pub world, in the middle of the last century the Victoria Park Hotel advertised that it had '... a bowling green and an American bowling alley'.

There are records of several pubs in Yorkshire called the Four Alls, but Sheffield went one better with a pub in Infirmary Road called the Five Alls: the lawyer, I plead for all; the parson, I pray for all; the soldier, I fight for all; the Queen, I reign over all; and John Bull, I pay for all. Other pubs with interesting and unusual names included the

Q in the Corner in Paradise Square; whilst no obvious reasoning can be given for its obscure name, it had the odd distinction of being a resort for blind fiddlers. The Burnt Tree Tavern took its title after a tree in the grounds was struck by lightning and left an appropriate address — Burnt Tree Lane. And at the Warm Hearthstone, customers were invited to dip their own bread in the dripping from joints cooking over the pub fire!

The Lion and Lamb in Pea Croft is long gone but still remembered because of its famous sign:

'If the Lyon show'd kill the Lamb,
We'll kill the Lyon — if we can;
But if the Lamb show'd kill the Lyon,
We'll kill the Lamb to make a pye on.'

The modern pub called the Samuel Plimsoll on Chequers Row deserves mention for the man it celebrates. For while he made his name as a legislator and the man responsible for the safety line on ships which prevents their overloading, his background was in the beer business. His father, Thomas, was an excise officer in Sheffield, and Samuel's first job was as a clerk in Rawson's Brewery in Pond Street. He later moved to London, became Member of Parliament for Derby and in 1876 successfully introduced his Merchant Shipping Act which made him the friend of all seamen.

Friday the 11th March 1864 is writ large in the annals of Sheffield. It was this night that the great flood occurred, after an earth bank on Dale Dyke Reservoir collapsed following heavy rains for many days. The reservoir was high in Bradfield Dale to the north-west of the city, and millions of gallons of water spewed into Loxley Valley heading to the industrial area of the city. The tragedies were many but the inns and pubs seem to have suffered badly. (In a sense it was fortunate that the disaster happened at midnight after most of the customers had gone home.) A marker on the wall of a steel works to show how high the flood waters rose in the valley was seven feet off the floor.

The Rowell Bridge Inn at Loxley was the first casualty, but luckily the landlord was able to rouse his family and escape to the upper floors of an adjacent mill. (A workman in a nearby factory was, however, drowned.) But the inn was demolished and the landlord lost his entire stock of draught beer which was washed away, along with two pigs, one of which was recovered the next day. At Malin Bridge, the Malin Bridge Inn and the Stag were both destroyed and the residents drowned, although the nearby Yew Tree on higher ground escaped any damage.

There was severe damage to the Masons Arms where four people died, but a child in an attic bedroom was unaffected and slept through the tumult. Three pubs in Hillsborough were damaged and badly flooded. Others were flooded as the water reached towards the Wicker and the east end of the city. The Rose Inn at Hillsborough was not badly damaged, and was used on the following day both for laying out the bodies of the drowned and also for the coroner's inquests.

A pub that should never have existed stands tucked away in Victoria Street. It was built originally in 1867 as a shop and house in a small development, and had a clause in its lease that said:

'...property should not be used for business as an innkeeper, publican, beerhousekeeper, soap boiler, sugar baker...'

But by 1895 it had a beerhouse licence, although the first recorded use of its name, the Bath Hotel, came in 1908. Ind Coope of Burton-upon-Trent leased the Bath from Hooson Brothers of Sheffield from 1914 until 1920 when they bought it and nine cottages for £2,800. The name is taken from the nearby Glossop Street Baths.

Sheffield has a couple of haunted pubs. The Three Tuns in Silver Street Head is an unusual wedge-shaped building which is listed as of architectural interest. It was once the wash-house of St Vincents Convent and 'unexplained happenings' are said to take place in the cellar. The Ball in Darnell Road is reputed to be haunted by a barmaid who hanged herself from rafters in the attic.

During the Great War the practice of running what were known as 'tossing schools' started in Sheffield, with a good deal of heavy gambling attached to them. One man would throw five half crowns into the air and the betting would be on the proportion of heads to tails. The schools attracted large crowds, with gamblers coming from

The Bath Hotel in Victoria
Street should never have
existed.

all over South Yorkshire.

Pubs were used as information points as to where the next session would be held, and lookouts were posted to spot the approach of the police. Two gangs — the Mooneys and the Garvins — controlled the betting, taking a proportion of each bet struck. They were deadly rivals and between them were responsible for most of the organised crime in the city, including protection rackets.

There were fracas in many pubs, including the Nelson at Moorhead, the Queens Head in Pond Hill where the landlord had his face slashed by a razor, and the Barley Corn in Cambridge Street where Gus Platts, a former heavyweight boxing contender, was the landlord. Platts was known to have broken up several fights himself, but often accepted that discretion was the better part of valour.

In 1926 there was a terrible murder outside the Windsor Hotel in Attercliffe. Two members of the Garvin gang were tried and hanged for it and three others received jail sentences for manslaughter. The two Garvin brothers and George Mooney were also jailed for other offences. About the same time Percy Sillitoe, who was later to become head of MI5, was appointed Chief Constable of Sheffield. One of his first jobs was to rid the city of the mobs by creating the so-called 'flying squads' to give proper protection to pub landlords. He was remarkably successful: the Garvins were driven out of the city and Mooney become a respectable member of the community, much to the relief of many pub landlords.

At least nine pubs and two breweries in Sheffield never traded again as a result of the damage caused by the bombs of the Luftwaffe on the nights of the 12th and 15th December 1940. The blitz completely destroyed the Rawson Brewery in Pond Street, and the Anchor Brewery in Cherry Street was so badly damaged that it shut down production. Two other breweries survived unexploded bombs on their premises.

The worst of the pub disasters was at the London Mart in Fitzalan Square. It was known to most people as 'Marples' after an early landlord. (This is also the name given to today's rebuilt version.) When the air raid came, most of the drinkers and staff took to the cellars on the assumption that they would be safe there. Unfortunately the pub suffered a direct hit by a high explosive bomb and about eighty people were interred in the rubble. Miners helped in the rescue attempts but only four people were taken out alive.

When the agriculturalist Arthur Young visited the North of England in 1760, one of the places he went to was Rotherham. He was obviously not best pleased with his accomodation there, for he recorded in his diary:

'Rotherham. Crown. Very disagreeable and dirty. Hashed venison, potted mackerel, cold ham, cheese and melon, 1s.'

He was not an easy man to please, for on the same journey he found the Old Kings Arms in Leeds had a dirty cook and no beer, and near Castle Howard there was 'an excellent house, but dear and a saucy landlady'! In fairness to the Crown, when Sir Albert Richardson wrote his *The Old Inns of England* 170 years later it was one of a dozen or so pubs in Yorkshire that he recommended. What Young would have made of Rotherham 200 years later is hard to say. What he would have found is that most of the pubs now belong to the Bass empire following takeovers of the town's two breweries, Bentleys and Mappins, along with their tied estates.

However, some fine pubs remain with interesting tales to tell. The Belvedere on Moorgate Road was built in the 1830's and its original use as the local watch tower probably makes it unique amongst pubs of the county. The many-roomed Bridge Inn on Chantry Bridge, although looking historically good, has been discounted as the first on this site after an examination of old photographs. The unusually named Feoffees in Moorgate is on the site of a former school for the poor that was built in 1776; 'feoffees' being the trustees or guardians responsible for land usually held by a charity.

The County Borough in Bridgegate is one of the town's older pubs, dating from 1859 when it was called the Restaurant Inn. Rotherham acquired county borough status in 1902 but the name change came about twelve years later. It was originally owned by Mappins Brewery, which built the Cross Keys in Moorgate Street and the Foljambe Arms in Doncaster Road in the period between the wars. They are both good examples of the 'improved' style of public house with many rooms and lavish amenities, and luckily have been little changed. Money, it seemed, was no object in those days.

Along Westgate there are several pubs displaying the sign of Stones of Sheffield (now part of Bass), but the Cutlers Arms is one of the few that actually belonged to that brewery and was not taken over in the 1950's. It dates from 1903 and is said to have a ghost.

The Dusty Miller at the end of Westgate was built in 1895 to a curious wedge-shaped design. It is a former Bentley's pub, as is the impressive Phoenix Hotel in the town centre which still retains an exterior advertising sign for 'Bentleys (Rotherham) Beers'. Another is the Woodman in Midland Road which can date back to at least 1867, for there are records of coroner's inquests there and to hold them on licensed premises became illegal in that year.

On Boxing Day an ancient sword dance is performed outside the Old Harrow Inn at Grenoside. The leader of the dancers wears a 'rabbit' hat which is removed when the rest of the team create a knot of swords. At this he falls dead but the 'magic' of the dance brings him back to life again. There are two Red Lions in Grenoside. The Old Red Lion on the former coaching road could well be sixteenth century. It is known as the 'top lion', whereas the Red Lion, which dates from 1634, was built for the 'new' turnpike which is now the main A61 Sheffield to Barnsley road.

The historic village of Wentworth was once part of the estate of the Fitzwilliams, and the George and Dragon can date itself back 400 years although the site has origins in the thirteenth century.

At Swinton the Ship Inn is said to be haunted by a landlord who died whilst working behind the bar. His ghost is said to pull pints, flush toilets, turn off lights, wander around the pub and occasionally leave a glass upturned on the bar after taking a drink. (It was enough to make one landlady leave the place!)

The Strafford Arms at Stainborough has its own tiny cricket pitch. The house was once owned by the Earl of Strafford and dates from the early eighteenth century. Joseph Bramah was born at Stainborough in 1748 and he deserves a mention in any book connected with public houses, for he invented the 'manual beer engine' — the handpump — which has little changed to this day. He was a prolific inventor and amongst other things designed the machine for numbering Bank of England notes. There is also a Strafford Arms at Wakefield and at Hoyland Nether, although all three probably predate the creation of the earldom in 1847 and would have had earlier names.

The Union Hotel at Platts Common — demolished in 1964 — is still remembered for its splendid maroon and green tiled facade. At the turn of the century it housed a well-established small brewery which supplied the Union as well as a number of other local houses owned by the landlord and brewer, Samuel Banner. He advertised 'If you wish to preserve your health drink...UNION ALES', and mentioned that he had won six gold medals in brewing exhibitions.

The inns of Silkstone appear to have attracted customers with a poetic bent, for two of its pubs have had verses showered upon them. The sign of the Angel contained:

'Faith and Grace this house doth keep,
And Angel guards the door.
Faith is dead, the Angel fled,
And Grace is now no more.'

And over the fireplace of the Six Ringers could be seen the following cry of the heart from a former landlord:

'Customers came and I did trust them,
I lost my liquor and my custom.
To losses them both it grieved me sore,
So I'm resolved to trust no more.
Chalk is useful, say what you will,
But chalk ner paid the malsters bill.
I strive to keep a decent tap,
For ready money but no strap.'

The Cubley Hall at Penistone was built in Victorian times as a country house for the owner of the local engineering company. He was a member of the Cammell family which linked up with the Lairds to form the famous Clydeside shipbuilding firm. It is a mass of ornate plasterwork, mosaic tiled floors, stained glass and original woodwork.

Barnsley was a famous brewing town, with the Barnsley Brewery Company and its famous Oakwell Ales taking the dominant spot with an estate that included 260 pubs when it was taken over by John Smiths of Tadcaster in 1961. As far back as 1875, steam traction engines were delivering beer in the town and often being fined for exceeding the speed limit of four miles per hour. (The owners welcomed the fines on the basis that they were proof of the fast delivery service!) The incorporation of the company came about in 1888 at the Kings Head Hotel which was in Market Hill.

One of the Barnsley Brewery houses, the Manx Hotel in Sheffield Road, is thought to be the oldest trading pub in the town, but there is a claim on behalf of the Travellers, once known as the Three Travellers, in Shambles Street; this may well be because it is the only one remaining out of twelve pubs that were in the street in 1888.

The Royal Hotel in Church Street is well-established. It was built in 1740 as a private house but later became a coaching house called the White Bear. It was here that the first meetings of the Barnsley Canal Company were held, and it was used for the opening day celebrations in 1780. The present name was taken after a visit to the town by Queen Victoria.

The Queens Hotel in Regent Street was another that changed its name after the royal visit; it was owned by the brewery of James Fox and Son of Crowle on the Isle of Axholme. (The Barnsley Brewery Company took it over with some forty houses in 1949.) Fox had other pubs in Barnsley, including one at 87 Sheffield Road. It was a pub from 1825 and changed its name successively from the Hussar to the Ship Inn to the Sailor Prince and finally to the George, until it closed in 1911 to become two shops.

The Royal Oak in Queen Street was demolished in 1962 to make way for a large store. In the late nineteenth century it was owned and run by John Harvey who also brewed his own beer. He was obviously proud of it and proclaimed that it was:

'The ONLY HOUSE in Town for Ye Good Old English ALE..... A good and wholesome beverage brewed in Ye good old style on the premises from Pure Malt and Hops only.'

He had a rather clever trade mark of R V, being a pun on his own name and the reverse of Victoria Regina.

A couple of Barnsley pubs attract attention because of their names. The Gyngleboy in Cheapside is modern, but the name is medieval, being slang originally for a coin and later for someone who rattles or jingles coins in their pockets. The Tom Treddlehoyle at Pogmoor is named after Charles Rogers, a local author of the early nineteenth century who used it as his pen-name. Treadles were used to operate machines for weaving in 'cellar-hoyles' or sweatshops.

Darfield, five miles along the Doncaster road from Barnsley, deserves a mention not only because it was my birthplace but the

Cross Keys was also the first pub at which I ever had a drink of beer. It stands opposite the splendid parish church of All Saints (where I was christened) and from which it is said there was once a connecting passageway — though for what reason I cannot imagine, unless some wayward curate used it to sneak across for a pint. When I drank there quite illegally in my early teens it belonged to the Melbourne Brewery of Leeds. That was the start of a love affair that ended nearly twenty years later when Tetleys took them over. The present pub is modern, but the one I often reflect on was eighteenth century with low ceilings, flagged floors and wooden settles — the stuff that dreams are made of. In the churchyard is the grave of Ebenezer Elliot, the corn law rhymer who formed the Anti-Bread Tax Society. There may be a moral in all this!

HULL AND HOLDERNESS

'...Hull, though a sea-port, a place that I shall always look back to with delight.'
William Cobbett

John Taylor the water poet visted many inns in his time, mainly in the south of England, but he recorded a visit to Hull in the early seventeenth century when he stayed at the Kings Head. At the time, George Pease was the landlord:

'Thanks to my loving host and hostess Pease,
There at mine inn each night I took mine ease;
And there I got a cantle of Hull cheese.'

Taylor explains:

'Hull cheese is much like a loaf out of a brewer's basket — it is composed of two simples, mault and water, in one compound, and is cousin germane to the mightiest ale in England.'

'He hath eaten some Hull cheese' is one of the politer ways of saying someone is drunk, along with such contemporary classics as 'He hath seen the French King' and 'He hath been bit by the barn-weasle'. Tom D'Urfey's *Pills to Purge Melancholy* contains a poem *In Praise of Hull Ale* which can be sung to the tune of 'Greensleeves'; and Samuel Pepys is said to have drunk Hull ale in 1660.

Mug houses were popular in early eighteenth century Hull — particularly amongst the political factions — although the Tories appeared to have campaigned against them in the election of 1713. Mug houses were where individual mugs or tankards were hung over the bar, in the windows or even outside ale houses to await their owners. A contemporary record describes their atmosphere:

'Th' Whig Mug House is in White Friar Gate — downe what is call'd "Mug House Entry". This Entry is aboute 5 foote wide an' aboute a score o' strides long. At th' extreme, is an olde Ale House wi' th' signe-borde of a "Quart Mug" over th' Doorsteade, an' is kepte by a man, called Benjamin Gaskin, or "Sancho Ben" for a Nick name. Th' Whig gentlemen yn Hull as well as th' other spotts begun to forme these Nests yn diff'rente parts o' the' Town. Another is in Trinity House Lane, another in Low Gate, as well as one on th' Sewerside. At thes' Dens — what yy calle "Free an' Easy" clubbs are heldid, so yt th' Whig supporters can take theyre Mug o' Ale, talke Politicks, mak speaches, play Cardes, Merrils, Knacks an' other Hande Games; as well as talke over th' merits o' Candidates at futur' Elections.'

Later, as in London, the popularity of the mug houses was to wane, giving way to the more conventional local ale houses, city centre taverns and political clubs.

It is in the old town of Hull that the most interesting pubs can be found. Two hundred years ago there were fifty inns, alehouses and pubs in narrow High Street, now there is just one, the Black Boy. It was first mentioned in 1331 and has a fascinating history. Two tunnels were said to lead from here: one was built during the Civil War and led to the church; the other to the riverside was built by smugglers. And, of course, it is haunted. The ghost is friendly and usually appears well-dressed in a top hat and white pantaloons. In its time this four storey, narrow building has had many lives. It was once a private residence, at another time a corn merchant had his premises here, for a period it was a brothel and later wines and spirits and coffee were sold from here. In its early days as an inn during the eighteenth century cockfighting took place at the back. But it was a tobacconist who gave the place its present name when he used a young African as a doorboy and advertising gimmick. The front smoke room contains some excellent leaded lights and a carved fireplace with the Black Boy motif.

The Old White Hart in Silver Street is probably the oldest building in the city, dating from the middle of the sixteenth century. It was here in 1642 in the first floor parlour of what was then his residence or palace that the Governor of Hull, Sir John Hotham, took the decision to refuse Charles I entry to the city by barring the gates aginst him.

The Old White Hart on Silver Street in the 1930's.

King Charles is said to have waited five hours before declaring Sir John a traitor and moving on to Beverley. The carefully preserved 'plotting parlour' is panelled with some excellent masonic carvings. It is said that this is 'where the Civil War started'.

The building was badly damaged by fire in 1790 but stayed a private house until it was first licensed after substantial alterations in 1881. Various things have been found there, including some swords from the Civil War and, in the 1930's, a secret room was discovered with a skeleton of a woman and the skull of a child in it. And a 100 year old bottle of Guinness was found in a cupboard and is said to be haunted. Move the bottle and all sorts of odd things occur!

There is another pub nearby in Alfred Gelder Street called simply the White Hart, built by the former Hull Brewery in Edwardian days as one of several genuine gin palaces in the city. It is opulent and full of interest with, in particular, a magnificent ceramic horseshoe bar in the front room (which has great similarity to that in the tap room of the Garden Gate in Leeds) and an ornate frontage with a balcony.

The George in the Land of Green Ginger is reputed to be the oldest continually licensed pub in Hull, probably dating from 1449. In former times it was much larger than it is today, but one of its older fascinations still remains. What is claimed to be the smallest window in Hull is in fact a spyhole through which the night porter could watch for the arrival of coaches, and so have the welcome mat out by the time the guests made their entry to the inn. The name is not a royal one — the first of the Georges reigned in the early eighteenth century — but is taken from the Guild of St George.

Another old pub is the Bonny Boat in Trinity House Lane. It takes its name from an eskimo kayak brought back from a whaling expedition to the Arctic by Captain Andrew Barker in 1612. (Presumably someone said: 'that's a bonny boat'.) It has been carefully preserved and is in the Hull Maritime Museum. More history was remembered by an inn called the Lion and Key after the 'British Lion' — the Duke of Wellington — captured Ciudad Rodrigo or the 'Key of Spain' in 1812. The sign of this pub showed a lion with a key in its paw, and there is evidence that similar signs were around in the seventeenth century.

Some excellent Georgian pubs remain in Hull, but others have been lost because of insensitivity on the part of the authorities and the changing economic needs and purposes of the city. The Leicester Hotel in Mytongate, dating from 1791, was sadly demolished in 1979 after the Department of the Environment refused to allow it to be listed as a building of architectural and historic interest, which would have given it a certain amount of protection.

On Victoria Pier the excellent and unspoilt Minerva stands opposite where the Humber ferryboats left from, and is also close to the river pilots' base. It was built in 1809 on reclaimed land and by 1830 was being used as a hotel to cater for the continental trade (its staff were required to speak both French and German). The interior is little altered, including a tiny snug that seats just four

The staff at the Minerva on the waterfront had to be trilingual.

people but which was once a ladies' toilet. These days the Minerva has its own brewery with the appropriately named 'Pilots' Pride' as the house beer. Nearby the nineteenth century Oberon is one of many pubs in Hull named after a ship and yet another which claims a resident ghost.

The sixteenth century Humber Tavern at Paull, which rests alongside the river some six miles east of Hull, had a function in 1836 that must surely be unique to a public house — it was also a lighthouse. The area needed a light and the Trinity House Commissioners recognised this. They resolved:

'...that lights be exhibited in the windows of a public house at Paull as a temporary expedient until the erection of permanent lights in the neighbourhood under the direction of the committee for surveying the Humber.'

In the account book for the period is an entry:

'To James Tindale four weeks rent for a room in his house, the Humber Tavern at Paull, used for the purpose of establishing a light therefrom for the benefit of vessels navigating the River Humber — £2.'

Inland of Paull is Hedon, which at one time was also on the river and had its own 'haven'. It was the busiest port on the Humber and one of England's smallest and oldest boroughs (its charter dates back to 1348). In 1774 the Hedon Haven Commissioners were established and their meetings were held in local inns, where they transacted their business and drank punch of a secret recipe. Reports say some of them were so drunk afterwards they were carted home afterwards in wheelbarrows by their servants. The Haven Commissioners still exist as a charitable trust and still drink punch, but these days are eminently respectable.

In Parliamentary terms, Hedon was a 'rotten' borough. It returned two members to the House of Commons although most of its small electorate lived elsewhere. At election times, 'treating' — the buying of drinks and meals to secure votes — was rife. Vast sums of money were spent to gain votes at both the Sir Charles Saunders Inn — now renamed the Shakespeare but then named after a local MP — and the Tiger Inn, which has since been converted into the local post office. The Queens Head, a listed building, dates from 1780 and was once the town's principal coaching inn.

This was an area for smugglers and the 400 year old Crooked Billet at Ryhill was a haunt of theirs. What are now the toilets in this pub was once a slaughterhouse. The Nancy at Burton Pidsea is yet another Yorkshire pub which takes its name from a successful, locally-bred racehorse. In 1851 Nancy, which was stabled at the Rose and Crown in Beverley, won twelve out of its thirteen races, including the prestigious Chester Cup.

Easington stands at the entrance to Spurn Point and has three very old inns. The Neptune, the Marquis of Granby and the White Horse are all more than 400 years old. The Neptune is a listed building of great character with cobbled walls, a feature of the area. The Plough

The Neptune at Easington has unusual cobbled walls.

Inn at nearby Hollym is the only inn of wattle and daub construction left in Holderness.

The unusually-named Gote Gate Inn in Withernsea is from about the same period, and is certainly the oldest pub in this small seaside town. It has recently reverted to a form of its original name after being called the Alexandra since 1938. Before 1866 it was a farm called Got Gate House, a name Danish in origin with 'gote' or 'got' meaning a drain, ditch or stream, and 'gate' meaning a road or way. It retained the name when it became a pub until 1938, when its present splendid sign was painted for Hull Brewery who had just acquired it. It shows a goat, but the artist said that this was merely to add life to the picture and the other elements — a way over a stream — reflected the original name.

The stories about the highwayman Dick Turpin are legion. Of those that link him to inns, there are two principal ones connected with his arrest, his subsequent trial in York and his execution. One claims that he was arrested in the Blue Bell at Beverley (now called the Beverley Arms), and the other says it was at the Green Dragon at Welton some ten miles west of Hull that he was apprehended. Both are plausible and both have many threads in common.

Merely because there is a discrepancy about the date, the Beverley story takes precedence chronologically. It is said that in 1738 the horse he was riding — which had previously been stolen — was spotted. It was a black gelding with a small white star on its forehead. (The highly fictional 'Black Bess' perhaps?) Turpin, or John Palmer as he was calling himself, was arrested and sent to York for trial. He wrote to his brother in Essex asking him to stand bail but, being of a mean nature, he failed to pay the carriage of the letter. His brother refused to accept it and it was sent back to the postmaster, who was also Turpins's former teacher and recognised his writing. He did whatever the medieval equivalent was of 'shopping' the highwayman, who stood trial under the name of Turpin at York and was hung at the Knavesmire in April 1739.

The Welton story, which appears to have more adherents, is set a year later, and the Green Dragon displays a facsimile record of his arrest for stealing horses in Lincolnshire. He is said to have forded the beasts across the Humber, hauled up at the inn for the night, got drunk, shot a gamekeeper and was arrested. At this stage it was discovered he was Turpin and not Palmer, and was wanted for highway robbery at Hampstead in North London. He was sent to York for trial and the two stories then enjoin.

Of course there are variations to both tales. One has it that the Green Dragon was a regular haunt of Turpin; that there is a trapdoor where he made his escapes from the Bow Street Runners; and that there is a window through which he leapt through on to the back of Black Bess! Another says that on the night of his arrest he went beserk and shot some poultry and then threatened their owner.

According to Denzil Batchelor in his book *The English Inn* there are eight inns in Yorkshire that claim to be the one in which Turpin had his last drink. (The Blue Boar in York was where his body was placed until his burial in St George's churchyard.) There are other tales about his relationship with drinking houses. Turpin was born the son of an innkeeper at Hempstead in Essex and he almost certainly killed his friend, Tom King, in the yard of the Red Lion in Whitechapel.

Many of Turpin's exploits ought more properly to be debited to another highwayman, John Nevison — called 'Swift Nick' by Charles II — who did ride from London to York in a remarkably short time to establish an alibi. He was arrested in the Three Houses Inn at Sandal near Wakefield and executed at York in 1684, twenty-one years before Turpin was born.

The Beverley Arms Hotel at North Bar Within (then the Blue Bell) was well-established by 1666 when the Garter King at Arms, Sir William Dugdale, held his Herald's Visitation there. The gentry from all over the East Riding came there to register their coats of arms with the College of Heralds. It was rebuilt in 1700 and again in 1790 when its name was changed. It has a famous kitchen which at one time had five fireplaces This room attracted the attentions of Fred Elwell, a local Royal Academician, whose paintings of it hang in the Tate Gallery and the Walker Art Gallery in Liverpool. It has now been converted into a lounge.

Many famous politicians have stayed at the Beverley Arms over the years, for this was the Tory inn in Beverley. It was a tradition for their candidate at General Elections to address an eve-of-poll meeting from the balcony over the door, and again when he was elected — as he usually was. The balcony led from the long assembly room on the first floor in which the party faithful would celebrate their victory.

There are claims that Anthony Trollope lodged here during the 1868 General Election when he was the Liberal candidate for Beverley. This is unlikely, and it seems the Angel was a more likely accomodation for him, as its flamboyant landlord Daniel Boyes once led a mob in a raid on the Tory committee rooms. Mr Boyes also had culinary skills — he once baked a pie for a New Year's feast that weighed ten stones and fed thirty-five people.

In the seventeenth century the town bellman would call out 'Cockin' tonight at eight, at the Bay Horse in Lairgate'. Cockfighting was popular, and despite legislation in 1654 to prohibit it the practice continued openly into the nineteenth century. (There was even a prosecution in Beverley for allowing cockfighting as recent as 1982.) But in other respects it was a law-abiding town and one of the last in Britain to prohibit Sunday drinking, for up to 1853 the church-wardens would patrol the town, visiting the inns to catch out landlords who allowed the practice.

Not everybody in the town would know where the White Horse is, but most if not all could tell you that 'Nellie's' is in Hengate. They are in fact the same pub. It was kept by the Collinson family for eighty years from 1895, with Nellie being the last of the line. It remains gas-lit, although when Samuel Smiths of Tadcaster acquired it from the Collinsons in 1976 they found repairs to the gas pipes in the cellar made with chewing gum and candles laying alongside!

'Nellie's' is a maze of rooms with iron ranges and open fires. It dates from the fifteenth century, and although it may not have been a pub for all that time it was one of the town's principal coaching inns. There is a well in the yard and its sign is a rocking horse above the door. Only after Samuel Smiths moved in was a proper bar built; prior to that service had been from a table in a small kitchen. Nellie had a live-in lover known affectionately as 'Suitcase Johnny' — from the number of times she kicked him out of the place!

The nearby Royal Standard, built in 1546 on North Bar Within, is another pub which has had one family in control for many years. The Wildes held court there for exactly a century, and the nickname 'Dolly's' for the small back bar came from Dolly Wilde, landlady for thirty-four years. It was refronted during the eighteenth century and at various times has been known as the Boot Hotel and the Turf Hotel, the latter name reflecting a long association with horseracing.

There are other old pubs in the town, including the Green Dragon, dating from 1671 and originally called the Malt House, that was once the town house of the Warton family; and the Kings Head, a Georgian coaching house which is said to be haunted. Both are in the Saturday market. Part of the Sun, which is close to the Minster, probably dates from the middle of the sixteenth century — it may well be the oldest inn in Beverley — and is said to be haunted by monks.

Beverley is another town with a long poem containing all the names of its inns and pubs. The author is unknown, which is perhaps as well for the rhyme and metre leave much to be desired:

> 'I met a man the other day
> With Rose and Crown in hand
> When all at once he made a stop
> And under Beverley Arms did stand
> The Royal Standard waved over him
> Like a Valiant Soldier he then stood
> He mounted on a grand White Horse
> But not one made of wood.'

— and so on for another eight verses, mentioning old and new houses and alternative names for some of them, until:

> 'We went down to the Railway
> When brightly shone the Sun
> Then all at once I spied the Dog and Duck
> So I went and fetched my gun
> When I came back I found the dog
> Was up the old Oak Tree
> So I shipped on a Sloop near Beverley Beck
> And sailed away to sea.'

At one time there were several ferries across the Humber, but the last one closed when the Humber Bridge opened. Invariably they were served by inns on both sides of the river. The Ferryboat Inn was the departure point for the ferry from Hessle and the Ferry Inn at Boothferry served two ferries, a small punt for people and a larger barge for animals and carriages. The Cottingwith ferry across the Derwent had the Ferry Boat Inn on the west side and the Bluebell on the east.

Goole is a company town, planned with precision in the early nineteenth century to become the major inland port of England. A Dutchman, Cornelius Vermuyden, undertook massive land drainage works, including the 'Dutch River' which links the town with the River Don. There is a pub named after him on the banks of the 'river' he built. On Aire Street there are three historic pubs, including another that is named after one of the town's founding fathers; the Macintosh Arms remembers Hugh Macintosh who commissioned the building of Goole Docks. Next door is the Royal Hotel, which started life in 1841 as a theatre to become a pub around the turn of the century.

Opposite stands the Lowther Hotel, the oldest standing building in Goole. It was built by the Aire and Calder Navigation Company as a coaching house to link with steamers on the Ouse from Hull, and was then called Banks Hotel. Its present name honours Sir John Lowther who was chairman of the company for many years. On the first floor in what was once the boardroom is a Victorian mural depicting the life and industry of the town in its heyday.

The origins of the sign of the Dog and Duck is not as cosy as one would expect. The one at Walkington reflects a barbaric pastime of spaniels chasing tethered ducks in a village pond. The only recourse the bird had was to dive to avoid the dogs. This 'royal diversion of duck hunting', as it was called, gave its name to several river and pond side inns. The Barrel is the smallest of the village's three pubs, and Ivan Broadhead in his book on Humberside says it is the geographical centre of that newly-created and unloved county.

One of the most attractive villages in the East Riding is Bishop Burton. Its duck pond and church on the hill overlook the Altisidora, yet another inn named after a winning racehorse. Richard Watt owned much of the land in the area, including the former Horse and Jockey inn which he had recently renamed Evander after another of his horses. But Altisidora was his pride and he backed heavily on it to win the St Leger in 1813 which, fortunately for him, it did and once more the name of the inn was changed.

The name of the Pipe and Glass Inn at South Dalton is a simple reflection of the pleasures available within. It is possibly fifteenth

The George and Dragon at Aldbrough pictured in the late 1930's. It was an important coaching inn, but its antecedents date from long before these days and it was a village inn in the sixteenth century.

century and stands on the site of the former gatehouse to Dalton Park. Visitors to the house were afforded hospitality and accommodation here. Daltonholme was the seat of the Hotham family and the pub is the only part of the village not within the estate. (Sir John Hotham was the Governor of Hull who refused the keys of the city to Charles I.) The pub was recently badly damaged by fire.

There has been an inn at Brandesburton since the early sixteenth century on the site where the present-day Dacre Arms stands, which dates from 1806. It was an important posting house and had stabling for fifty horses. The justices held court there and it had its own brewery. In the original building there was a lattice window that contained 150 pieces of glass. The pub had a secret room with a trap door where fugitives from the 1745 Rebellion were hidden, and where smugglers kept their contraband.

In 1844 the Franklin Dead Brief was formed at the Dacre. This was a mutual benefit society similar to many others that were being set up about that time. Its rules were very simple and still apply today: it was four shillings to join, of which half went to the general funds and the other half to the estate of the next member to die; and each member paid four shillings on the death of another. The annual meeting is held at the Dacre Arms on the first Wednesday in February, and the pub landlord is always the treasurer. Presently there are 270 members.

The Londesborough Arms at Market Weighton is another example of a local family marking the map by naming inns and pubs after themselves. (There are other inns called 'Londesborough' at Seamer and Selby, but the one at Tadcaster has been renamed.) It was a coaching inn but now serves the market and the farming community, and still provides accomodation for travellers. Nicholas Pevsner in his *Buildings of England* series said it was the only house in the town with some 'cachet'.

The Alice Hawthorn at Weldrake recalls the champion mare of the 1840's, which has one of the most amazing records in racing. Three generations of Boltons kept this pleasant village pub and they were all called Fred. One of them explained how he thought the horse got its name. It came, he said:

'...from a mare that had a foal in a field nearby under a hawthorn bush and was found by a lass called Alice, and it won a big race and war a champion, it war...'

There is another tale that it was called after the owner's mistress. Why the pub took the name of the horse is easy to understand, for between 1841 and 1845 it won 51 of its 71 races, deadheated in another and was placed in 10 of the rest. Amongst its prizes it won sixteen cups. There is a similarly-named pub at Nun Monkton to the north of York.

The 300 year old St Vincent Arms at Sutton-upon-Derwent is part of the St Vincent estate. The first viscount, Admiral Sir John Jarvis, was responsible for the defeat the French at Cape St Vincent in 1801. Originally it was two cottages, and when it was rebuilt and extended, timbers from one of the admiral's men o' war were used.

The Feathers in Pocklington has had ghosts and political scandals.

The Feathers in Pocklington's market place is an imposing inn which has serviced the town's market and provided stabling for farmers for nearly four centuries. It was also a coaching inn and managed to preserve this facility well into the present century. The coach parties of Samuel Ledgard, which ran from the Nelson Inn at Leeds, called here for refreshments on their way to Bridlington. The Feathers Field behind the inn was used to stage horse and cattle fairs in May and at Martinmas. The pub has a fascinating history. Public hangings took place in the yard — the most famous of which when the hangman himself was executed. There is inevitably a ghost, not of the hangman but of a highwayman who murdered a serving maid from the Feathers in 1810. Since then the room in which it took place is said to have 'an atmosphere'. Often guests refuse to sleep there after one night. There are reports of them hearing heavy breathing, and other noises as if someone was dragging a large object across a floor.

But it was a political scandal in 1834 for which the Feathers is best-known. (No doubt today it would hardly raise a column inch in the local paper.) It was the Tory inn of the town and Lord Brougham — the Lord Chancellor and a Whig — was travelling by chaise from York to Hull with his daughter and secretary. They broke their journey at the Feathers and claimed that they had been shoddily treated.

The Yorkshire papers split into two camps according to their political views, the Whig papers saying that Lord Brougham's reception included no fire in the room and no breakfast available, even though the landlord had been notified of their coming. One paper even suggested that there were no horses available in the town. The landlord was supported by the Tory press, which claimed that no breakfast had been ordered, only a change of horses, and that the party had arrived two hours early.

The Feathers won the day, and an apology was published by one paper which said:

'It is well known to all travellers through Pocklington that at the Feathers Inn, post-horses have been kept for the last half-century and we understand that there is no more accomodating establishment in the East Riding.'

Lord Brougham never visited Pocklington again!

Driffield — or Great Driffield to be more precise — is the capital of the Wolds and has some interesting pubs. One of the oldest, and still in business, is the Red Lion, which of late took the prefix 'Old'. It is next to the church and dates back three centuries. The justices held court there and it was also the village lock-up before the building of the police station.

The Keys Hotel was once a most impressive four storied inn, but two have now been removed; and the Buck Hotel displayed a bicycle wheel above its door to indicate that cyclists were welcome and could be accomodated. The Bell Hotel was the politicians' pub with a balcony above the door from which aspiring candidates could harangue the masses. It also maintained a horse and carriage which transferred guests between the hotel and the station, which was known affectionately as the 'Bell Bus'.

The Anvil Arms at Wold Newton was previously called the Crooked Billet, and had an unusual sign of an untrimmed stick hanging over the door and a signboard with a verse on either side. On one:

'When this comical stick grew in the wood,
Our ale was fresh and very good.
Step in and taste, O do make haste,
For if you don't twill surely waste.'

— and on the other:

'When you have viewed the other side,
Come read this too before you ride.
And now to end we'll let it pass,
Step in, kind friends, and take a glass.'

YORK

'Yorke, Yorke, for my monie,
Of all the cities that ever I see,
For merry pastime and companie.'

Sixteenth century ballad

In a city of great antiquity, historic pubs and inns are an expectation. And so it is with York. From the thirteenth century onwards, the guilds of the city (which had craft, social or religious purposes) provided their own ale chambers and often accommodation for strangers and travellers. There has been an inn on the site of the present Cross Keys Hotel at Dringhouses since 1250, although the present building is early eighteenth century. There are others, too, which have traces of very old structures even though they have been much altered. Within the walls of the city the Olde Starre in Stonegate may well have fourteenth century origins, but the Black Swan in Peasholme Green is probably the oldest inn in York.

York's oldest inn: the Black Swan on Peasholme Green.

In the reign of Edward VI an Act of Parliament in 1552 determined the number of taverns in the major towns and cities of England. London was to have 40 and York 8, whilst others had smaller numbers; and in 1578 the magistrates ordered that 'all innkeepers in the city shall have at least six comely and decent bedrooms for guests'. At Acomb the manorial court declared: 'A tippler [innkeeper] shall not lodge any pedlars, tinkers or other vagrant persons without consent of the local constable.' Two centuries later a further act declared that all public houses should be registered, and in the next forty years the number in York dropped by a quarter. And in a case before the Grand Jury in York in 1787, reference was made to the '...evil of petty alehouses'.

The Black Swan is not only the oldest inn but the only one of several in the city that are listed as being of architectural and historic interest that holds a grade two 'star' rating, giving it additional protection against any insensitive alterations or demolition. A late sixteenth century building, it was the home of the Bowes family which gave Lord Mayors to both York and London. (Sir Martin Bowes presented York with its sword of state whilst he held the London office in 1545.) It is reputed to have been the birthplace of General James Wolfe, the hero of Quebec, but this is unlikely as most records show him as being born at Westerham in Kent. What is certain is that his mother lived here around 1700. Although there have been recent refurbishments, there are still some seventeenth century memories with a magnificent staircase, fireplaces and doorways. The oak panelling has some Biblical carvings and the timber-framed exterior is splendid, with its carved bargeboards.

Across Stonegate there is a sign for the Olde Starre Inn that stretches across the street — a 'gallows' sign that is unique in Yorkshire. The pub itself is tucked away down an alley. Whilst the living quarters have fourteenth century traces, the present-day layout is mainly late nineteenth century. It was then owned by the local brewery of Brett Brothers, although it was first noted as an inn in 1644. It remains full of splendid Victorian stained glass and mahogany panelling, with a superb bar screen. It seems to have more ghosts and hauntings than any other in Yorkshire. Two black cats disturb its peace and an old lady was seen by the child of a former licensee. Dogs have knocked themselves unconcious against the bar whilst going for an invisible opponent. And in the cellar can be heard the screams of victims of Civil War battles, who had their limbs amputated without the benefit of anaesthetic when the pub was used as a hospital.

The landlord at the time was William Foster, a Royalist, who had to preside over the celebrating Roundhead troops. A contemporary rhyme described his feelings:

> 'A bande of soldiers with boisterous dinne,
> Filled up large kitchen of ye Olde Starre Inne;
> Some rounde ye spacious chimney, smoking satt,
> And whiled ye time in battle talk and chat,
> Some at ye brown cake table gamed and swore,
> While pikes and matchlocks strewed ye sanded floore.
> Will Foster ye hoste, mid ye groupe was seene,
> With full redd face, bright eye and honest miene;
> He smoked in silence in his olde inn chaire,
> No jokes nor jestes disturbed his sadden'd air.'

The Red Lion in Merchantgate is a wonderful building which first saw life in the thirteenth century and has been a pub for more than 300 years. It is another for the list of 'Dick Turpin drank here' pubs.

A run of fourteenth century tenements at the top of Micklegate includes the Coach and Horses, another listed building. Some of the additions are seventeenth and eighteenth century but the inside is modern. It is usually known as the 'little coach', originally to identify from another similarly-named pub in Nessgate — the 'big coach' — but that one has now closed. There was also a Coach and Horses in Jubbergate, known as 'Saynors' after the family that owned it.

The Old White Swan in Goodramgate has parts which date from the fifteenth century, though first records of it as a pub were in 1703. It has been much altered over the years, but a recent renovation was sensitive and attempted to restore it to its former glory. It has the only

The Coach and Horses on Jubbergate was known as 'Saynors'.

The sign of the Old Black Swan.

remaining mounting steps in the city and a Roman column is preserved inside. In the same street the Anglers was also fifteenth century, although it was remodelled in 1920. (It is yet another pub with its own ghost.) And the Nags Head in Micklegate is a half-timbered listed building from 1530; it was refronted in the eighteenth century and retains an attractive bow window.

The first of York's inns to run a regular coach service to London was the Old Black Swan in Coney Street. A large store now stands on the site, but its excellently-preserved sign can be seen in the Castle Museum. As early as 1706 there were coaches running from here to the Black Swan in Holborn, and in its heyday it could stable 100 horses. The American author Nathaniel Hawthorne stayed there with his wife and son in 1857 after travelling to York from Leeds by train. He wrote:

'It is a very ancient hotel for in the coffee house I saw on the wall an old poster announcing that a stage-coach would leave the Black Swan in York (and travel to London) in four days dated 1706. It is a very good hotel.'

Another of Coney Street's lost inns is the George, but again there is a memory in the form of a sign outside the Leak and Thorp store:

'In Elizabethan times Ralph Rokeby Esquire (d. 1575) Secretary of the Council of the North, lived in a house on this site. Subsequently for about two and a half centuries there existed here a hostelry known since 1614 as the George Inn from which horsedrawn coaches departed to Hull, Manchester and Newcastle.'

The George — the principal posting inn of the city — is also remembered by a column in the Herald building. John Taylor, the water poet, stayed here in 1622 after the epic journey in an open boat from London. He recorded in his *A very merrie, wherry-ferry voyage or York for my money* that he visted the archbishop and the Lord Mayor; he acknowleged the landlord of the George, Thomas Kaye, in the rhyming account of the trip:

'...to honest Mr Kayes in Cunnystreet.
He entertain'd me well, for which I thank him,
And gratefully amongst my friends I'll rank him.'

John Byng recorded in his *Torrington Diaries* that he visited the George in June 1792:

'...which inn is one of those very old houses whose front is adorn'd by stucco'd imagery and in it is a very grand apartment with much carved work; and stain'd glass in the windows. My landlord said that our house was formerly a mansion of the Duke of Buckingham, and was built upon the site of the Priory of St Leonards'.

Byng said he enjoyed a good dinner at the 'civil' inn, and kept a copy of his bill which showed that he paid one shilling and sixpence for his dinner and half a crown for wine. His total bill — which appeared to be for two nights — came to eleven shillings and eightpence. Other visitors included the architect Sir John Vanbrugh and the sisters Charlotte and Anne Brontë. Leak and Thorp moved on to the site in 1869.

Etteridges Hotel in Lendal has also vanished, although parts of it remain in Thomas's Bar. It was the staging post in York for gentlemen and noblemen travelling by post chaise or in their own private carriages. Tommy Etteridge was a 'character' and lived here all his life. He weighed twenty-four stone, drove around York every day in a gig and drank every evening in the Punch Bowl in Stonegate. At one time he called it 'Etteridges Royal Hotel' — although there is no evidence of royalty having visted it.

The York Tavern in St Helen's Square was regarded by some people as the most important of the inns of York. The mail coaches started from here and it was next door to the Post Office. It was bought by a Mr Harker who renamed it Harkers Hotel. He was a bloodstock dealer, kept a stud farm at Stillington and had horses in training at Malton.

Up to 1962 the Plumbers Arms stood in Skeldergate, but despite protests it was allowed — along with some other excellent buildings — to be demolished for road widening. It was the sort of insensitive action that was prevalent in those days: in a recent report by the York Civic Trust, which mentions its destruction along with that of the Queens Arms in Fossgate, there is a comment, '...they would never have gone today you may be sure'.

The origins of the Plumbers Arms were in 1575 when it was built as a merchant's house. It did not become a beerhouse until 1870 and was bought by John Smiths of Tadcaster in 1909. There is a good deal of confusion about its early history, but it does appear to have had connections with the Duke of Buckingham who may have used it as a laboratory. According to Larwood and Hotten in their *History of Signboards* it was once called Dukes Place, but it is more likely that this was a nickname — as is the Cock and Bottle, the title given to the pub that replaced the Plumbers in 1965. The new pub is said to be haunted by the second Duke of Buckingham whose glowing face appears above the fireplace!

In 1941 the Plumbers Arms was damaged during an air raid — fortunately not seriously with its only obvious casualty being a diamond-shaped pane of glass in one of the front windows. This has been restored and is preserved in its successor. It is inscribed and tells us a little of the history of the building by its dating:

'A

glazer I

Am and I

work for my

bred and many

fine window in my

time have I made

I with my diamond have

Cut out the Glass and

in a Corner Cist many

a prity lass 1789'

There are carved bargeboards on the Punch Bowl in Stonegate dated 1675. The pub was heavily restored in the 1930's, albeit most sensitively by its then owners the Tadcaster Tower Brewery. It is an excellent example of the 'Brewers' Tudor' style. It may well be due for further treatment, and one can only hope taste and common sense will prevail. It is a listed building and its splendid frontage fits well into what must be the most photographed street in York (although unfortunately it does lie back a little from the building line).

In a BBC television documentary made in 1985 I described the Fox in Holgate as '...a Victorian workingmen's boozer'. When it was rebuilt in 1878 that was exactly what it was, catering for the workers at the nearby railway carriage works. (It still does to some extent today.) But there had been a pub there before in a building that first saw life in the early eighteenth century as a private house or possibly a farm. Licensed in 1776, it was called the Cross Keys to reflect the badge of the Archbishop of York who owned the land. It became the Fox in 1843, and the rebuilding took place when the magistrates were showing concern about the standard of accomodation in licensed premises.

The landlord of the Fox in 1898, Thomas Robinson, bought the pub, farm buildings and some outbuildings for £7,000. Less than a year later he sold the pub and the outbuildings to Joshua Tetley's Brewery of Leeds for £16,200, retaining the agricultural side and carrying on with that business himself. The most recent refurbishment was in 1985 when it became a Tetley Heritage Inn. There was another Fox in Low Petergate which dated from the fifteenth century but it was demolished in 1958; at one time it was called the Beech Tree and later the Lord Byron.

In Market Street, the Hansom Cab is of seventeenth century origin, a listed building that was once known as the Burns Hotel. Its present name is taken from the light two-wheeled horse-drawn cab invented by Joseph Aloysius Hansom, who was born in York in 1803. He was also the architect of Birmingham Town Hall.

What is now called the Hole in the Wall in High Petergate by Bootham Bar was previously the Board Inn. It was one of many of that name in York and the derivation has several possibilities. Because there were many such inns in Scarborough and other holiday towns the most likely is a simple one — that they provided board and lodgings. Another, which may not contradict the first, is that they had a plain sign board. At least two others have been noted, though they are difficult to locate; one changed its name to the Old Number Five and the other to Gibsons Vaults.

The Hole in the Wall is built on the site of a debtors' prison and gets its present name from the hole through which food was passed to the inmates. It was largely rebuilt in 1982 when North Country Breweries of Hull bought it after it had been allowed to deteriorate, but its frontage remains intact.

At least ten inns and pubs in York appear to be named after successful racehorses, although some have long vanished and in other

cases the origin is questionable. They commemorate some remarkable horses. Charles XII won the St Leger and the Doncaster Cup
within three days in 1839, and its success in the former was in a re-run
after dead heating with Euclid. But not only did it run three races in
three days, it had been walked from York to Doncaster to take part
in them! The horse was named after a King of Sweden, a rash and
ambitious general whose ominous claim to fame was that he was
defeated by Peter the Great. The pub named after the horse is
at Heslington.

The Beeswing on the Hull road presently bears a sign of the racehorse of that name, although there is another theory that it is taken
from the name for the film that gathers on good port, and for a time
this pub had a bee in flight on its sign. The pub is older than the
racehorse and its reputation for fine old port dates back to the late
eighteenth century when it was probably called the Black Swan. The
horse named Beeswing was a contemporary of Charles XII and was
unbeaten between 1837 and 1842, when it won the Doncaster Cup
four times with a hat-trick from 1840 to 1842. It also won the Ascot
Gold Cup in 1842. There is a similarly-named pub at East Cowton
in the North Riding and there was once one in Sheffield. Another
doubt about the derivation of the name of all three pubs is thrown in
by the fact that there was another horse called Beeswing that won the
Liverpool Autumn Cup in 1866.

The Bay Horse in Monkgate was originally called the Bay Malton,
a horse which was said to have had a most distinguished career
between 1764 and 1767. Several other pubs are named after Classic
race winners. The Barefoot, which was in Micklegate, recalls the
St Leger winner in 1823; the Flying Dutchman, formerly known as
the Bloomsbury, is called after the winner of both the Derby and
the St Leger in 1849; and the recently-opened Brigadier Gerard
in Monkgate is in memory of one of the greatest of recent flat
champions, which included the 2,000 Guineas in 1971 amongst its
ten important wins.

The Eclipse, also once called the Black Swan, is no longer with
us. The horse won many races and the Eclipse Stakes at Sandown

Some of the racehorse inn signs in and around York.

was named after it. The Froghall was also a regular winner; the pub was in Layerthorpe.

Two others are still in business: the Old Ebor, a splendid Victorian pub in Nunnery Lane, is according to one record named after a race-horse; and the Tam O' Shanter in Lawrence Street may either be named after the horse that won the Chester Cup in 1876 or be a literary reference to Robert Burns's epic poem.

Development in the east end of the city outside the walls came about with the building of the cattle market and new barracks in Fulford Road. The Shire Horses, the Cattle Market and the Phoenix were all purpose-built pubs to serve the market (there were others, now vanished). The Light Horseman was built in 1830 at the same time as residences for the families of cavalry officers. It is high ceilinged and completely different to the neighbouring urban locals of the same period; the recent description of '...a handsome Victorian building...' is appropriate. The Wellington in Alma Terrace was

The Light Horseman in the east of the city is completely different to other nearby pubs of the same period.

purpose-built, and when Samuel Smiths bought it in 1887 it was described as 'an old established beerhouse'.

It is difficult to avoid pubs in York that are said to be haunted. The city council even runs its own 'Ghost Walk', which starts at the Anglers in Goodramgate. In the same street, excavations at the Golden Slipper showed up a hidden slipper which — romance has it — should never be moved, for it was placed there after the murder of a young bride and it wards off evil spirits. And the Exhibition in Bootham has what is called a 'friendly poltergeist'.

Through the Bar in Petergate is the York Arms, in a terrace designed in 1838. (Originally it was called the Chapter Coffee House.) Its ghost is a well-known one and shares its presence with other buildings in the area. It is another 'grey lady', in this case thought to be a nun who gave birth to a child and who was bricked up in a room as punishment. She is supposed to be searching for her lost child. The event took place on the site of the nearby Theatre Royal and she has been seen in several buildings round about. At the York Arms she has made her presence felt in many ways. A pile of ashtrays once showered over a landlady; a pair of bellows jumped ten feet from the wall; and another time someone was struck with an object that came through a closed door. One landlord threw a paint brush at the lady but it went straight through her.

Of a number of excellent late Victorian pubs in York, the Blue Bell in Fossgate stands out. According to the pub conservation group of York CAMRA it is '...the last perfectly surviving Victorian pub interior in York'. They go on to call it '...a little gem'. It has a small front bar in the West Riding 'shop style' and the back lounge is served through a curtained doorway. In the corridor — where drinking is encouraged — a tiny drop-down seat is an unusual feature. The glazed brick facade gives it an outstanding appearance, which Hutchinson and Palliser in their book *York* rather oddly describe as 'fierce'.

The Burton Stone Inn, once called the Plough, was built in 1896 by Walter Brierley, said to be 'one of the best three architects to have practised in the city'. It is on the site of an ancient inn — a reminder

The building of 'improved' public houses at the turn of the century is reflected in the Minster Inn along Marygate.

is the original 'burton stone' where travellers in plague times would cleanse their coins in vinegar before moving on. This and the nearby Minster Inn in Marygate are good examples of the burgeoning of the 'improved' public house. The architect here was C W C Needham who built it for the Tadcaster Tower Brewery in 1903. Its layout is simple, with a corridor, bar, smoke room and a back lounge that was intended as a coffee room.

On the green at nearby Clifton, in medieval times there stood a maypole and a pub named after this symbol of springtime. In the middle of the seventeenth century the Maypole was the scene of a double murder and of a fire — events that led to three women going to the gallows. First, two young sisters poisoned their lovers by putting oxalic acid in their ale and were duly convicted and hung at York in 1647. Then, two years later, another women was to hang for arson after she was convicted of burning down the pub. There is a claim that Ursula Southiel was born at Clifton — she is better known as Mother Shipton the prophetess — and a pub named after her can be found in Knaresborough where she lived for many years.

THE PLAIN OF YORK

'Now Northallerton, Thirsk and Easingwold — a famous trinity of Yorkshire market towns — are all within striding distance of one another on the Great North Road, and have always been famous for their inns and ale.'

A J Brown

On fast dual carriageway between Tadcaster and York stands the Wildman, a pub built in the inter-war years but with long antecedents. Its name is interesting, dating from Elizabethan times and with a similar derivation to the Green Man, the character who played the fool at pageants, feasts and fairs. Sometimes they dressed as Bacchus, the God of Wine, other times like Robin Hood or Jack in the Green; sometimes they were caged. There is a history of a place of refreshment on this site for centuries, and it was used by highwaymen as a place of refuge. The sign was that of a naked man, and when Queen Victoria once passed this way it was discreetly draped for the occasion. When it was rebuilt, flints, coins and lamps made out of bottles were found in the foundations.

The Ship Inn at Acaster Malbis was once the landing place for a ferry across the Ouse from Naburn. A former landlord displayed a sign:

'My honest friend, I tell you true,
Good ales sold here by Michael Drew.'

Mr Drew was a bookworm and little interested in the inn, despite his sign. In his garden he built a summer house from an old boat to which he repaired to read his books, and which his customers took to calling 'Mickey's Cave'.

Long Marston is close to the site of the Battle of Marston Moor where in 1644 the Royalist troops were defeated by Cromwell, marking the start of the Commonwealth. The Sun Inn precedes this event and was named after Edward VI, the Sun King. The pub has no specific ghost but takes it share of the many who reputedly haunt the area: these include Prince Rupert fleeing on horseback, Cromwell himself and numerous Royalist soldiers.

The Punch Bowl at Marton-cum-Grafton is the oldest building in the village and dates from 1556. It is timber-framed with pantiles, most attractive and listed by the Department of the Environment as being of historic and architectural interest. The eighteenth century Ship Inn at Aldborough replaced a previous inn on the site which dated from the fourteenth century. The present building used ships' timbers for beams and has quarry-tiled floors.

There are some claims to longevity amongst the inns of Borough-bridge, which had a fine position in the days of coaching and droving. The Black Bull dates from the thirteenth century — in its time it was a coaching inn and is said to be haunted. The Musketeer was originally the Mauleverers Arms and the coat of arms on its sign included three greyhounds, so it later became the Three Greyhounds and then the Grey Hounds Hotel. Much of the original inn was turned into shops.

Opposite is the Crown, which was built on the site of the manor house where in 1569 the meeting was held to terminate the Rising of the North. The Blue Bell at Kirby Hill was another coaching inn that had the special facility of a cell used for prisoners being moved to jail. The Three Arrows takes its name from the three Bronze Age standing stones in fields to the west of the town. They are between sixteen and twenty-two feet high and the heaviest weighs thirty-six tons. Legend has it that the Devil shot them from his crossbow at the early Christian settlement of Boroughbridge. They are one of the county's most famous prehistoric monuments.

The crossroads at Sandhutton — referred to by many people as 'Busby Stoop' — takes its name from the seventeenth century inn there. The origins of its name are gory and have their reminder in both a tangible form and a ghost. It recalls Tom Busby, a coiner, who was hung in chains there in 1702 after he had beaten up his father-in-law with a hammer after a row over money. He is said to haunt the area with a noose round his neck. There was a chair in the inn for many years which was supposed to be kept for Busby — and which spelled

The Busby Stoop chair. In 1702
Tom Busby slept in the chair after killing
his father-in-law. Before he died he
cursed anyone who sat in it.

disaster or even death to anyone else who sat in it. Its effect was such
that public demand made one landlord place it in the cellar; later it
was given to the Thirsk Museum, where it remains.

There is a record of an inscription on the window of an inn between
Boroughbridge and Northallerton, but unfortunately the place has
not been identified. It was said to have been written by a parson in the
early nineteenth century:

> 'Here in my wicker chair I sitt
> From folly far, and far from witt
> Content to live, devoid of care
> With country folk and country fare.
> To listen to my landlord's tale
> And drink his health in Yorkshire ale
> Then smoke and read the *York Courant*
> I'm happy and 'tis all I want
> Though few my tythes, and light my purse
> I thank my God it is no worse.'

According to Alfred J Brown in his *Four Boon Fellows* there is a grave in Northallerton churchyard for the one-time landlord of the Sun Inn, and on the stone it reads:

> *'Hic jacet* Walter Gunn
> Sometime landlord of the Sun.
> He drank hard upon Friday,
> That being a high day.
> Then took to his bed and died on Sunday.
> *Sic transit gloria Mundi!'*

The Sun receives a mention in *The Praise of Yorkshire Ale* which George Meriton wrote in 1685. This long, bawdy poem tells how Bacchus sets up his court in Northallerton prior to a journey to York to sample the ales of the county. It is fulsome in its praise of the town's ale:

> 'North-Allerton, in Yorkshire doth excell
> All England, nay all Europe for strong Ale.'

— and he goes on to use such terms as 'Nectar' and 'rare Ambrosia' for the copious amounts that were drunk in that alcoholic journey. No-one brews there today — although the Vale of Mowbray Brewery was at Leeming Bar until 1925 — but the town has a heritage of inns, being one of the most important coaching towns on the road from London through York to Edinburgh.

The first coaching inns were the Kings Head and the Black Bull, but the Golden Lion became the most important. It lasted beyond the coaching era whilst the other two closed and became shops. It is an impressive three storey eighteenth century building fronting on to the town's high street. The arch leads to what was once a yard running back more than a hundred yards. When the town had a horse fair, prospective purchases were galloped down it to show off their paces. It almost had a monopoly for post horses on the twenty mile stretch of road that took in Northallerton, and provided stabling for sixty of them as well as room for hunters and race horses at Northallerton Races.

The Reverend Sydney Smith — journalist, wit, and traveller — provided the Golden Lion with an unfortunate reputation for being

Northallerton's impressive Golden Lion Inn was the premier coaching inn
of the day, and survives to this day.

expensive. He gave it the fictitious name of the Black Swan and
advised:

'...not to set off too soon [from London] or you will be laid up at
the Black Swan, Northallerton, and your bill will come to a thousand
pounds.'

An advertisement in the *York Chronicle* in 1783 made another
oblique reference:

'...as the innkeepers of Northallerton have of late been so
extravagant in their charges.'

The landlord at this time was Francis Hirst, described as innkeeper,
coach proprietor and posting master. He entertained foreign royalty
in December 1815 and the local paper reported:

'The Grand Duke Nicholas and Constantine of Russia, accompanied by Sir William Congreve [not the dramatist], and a numerous
suite, in four carriages and four, and two outriders, arrived at Mr
Francis Hirst's Golden Lion Hotel, from York and stayed all night,
and proceeded next morning at eleven o' clock, on their tour to the
north. Mr Hirst set the whole off, with first rate horses and eight postboys, all dressed alike in scarlet and jockey caps.'

There was another, earlier, Golden Lion which took the prefix 'Old' — appropriately, for it is the oldest house in the town, although it is now called the Fleece. It was here in 1745 that John Wesley stayed and preached, and he is said to have found it charming.

Osmotherley is well known as the beginning of the forty mile Lyke Wake Walk across the moors to Ravenscar on the coast above Scarborough. The Queen Catherine is the starting point and it is here that the Winter Wake Dinner is held, where witches' broth and funeral biscuits are on the menu. (Catherine of Aragon, Henry VIII's first wife, built a chapel in the village.) The Kings Head was formerly called the Duke William after the Duke of Cumberland, the victor of Culloden, but it was renamed when he fell out of favour. And the Three Tuns dates from the seventeenth century. Amongst the many visitors to this historic village with its 'butter table' cross were Bonnie Prince Charlie on the march south, and John Wesley who preached here.

The Drover's Road goes south from Osmotherley as the alternative route to the Great North Road (the latter was a turnpike and so tolls were levied along it). The drovers came from Scotland and Northumberland with their cattle for the markets of the Midlands and the South, and because of the slow speed of their charges they needed to rest overnight every few miles and avoid the tolls. The Drover's Road had that provision. The Chequers at Slapestones was the first stop, with its famous enigmatic sign:

'Be not in haste, step in and taste,
Ale tomorrow for nothing.'

It had a peat fire which burned for more than 200 years, but sadly it closed as an inn in the 1920's.

Three miles south on the Black Hambleton was Limekiln House which ceased trading in 1890; and after a further five miles, Dialstone House, now a farm. It ceased to be an inn, in the words of a local, 'when a rather religious landowner took the licence away'.

The last of the Drover's Road inns is still with us: the seventeenth century Hambleton Inn stands guard at the summit of Sutton Bank, the steep road down to Thirsk.

The tantalising sign of the Chequers on the Drover's Road.

The Three Tuns in Thirsk's market place was its first coaching house — although it was built in 1698 as a dower house for the Bell family, changing in 1740 to a coaching inn for the London to Newcastle and Edinburgh and Leeds to Darlington services. However in 1815 the landlady retired and set up a relative in business at the nearby Fleece, later to be called the Golden Fleece. At one time the two inns between them could stable 200 horses.

The Fleece took over as the 'head' inn of the town and was said by the historian, Edmund Bogg, to be 'the most notable coaching inn between York and Darlington'. The Express coach which ran from London to Newcastle was worked on the Thirsk stretch by a one-eyed coachman called Peter Elliot. His team was led by a one-eyed horse and the other three were blind. It was jokingly said that where there should have been ten eyes there were only two!

There are tales told of the pubs in Easingwold back to the seventeenth century. In those days the White House at the north end of the town — now a private house — was a thriving tavern run by a man called Ralph Reynard. He wooed a servant girl but, after a tempestuous affair, they quarrelled and she left him to marry a farmer called Fletcher. The passion of the marriage soon cooled, the lady sought out her old love and an affair started which became the scandal of the area. Fletcher soon found out about it and set off for the White House. He was waylaid by Reynard and his ostler, Mark Duncan, the two drowned him and — with the help of Mrs Fletcher who was waiting nearby — buried him in the garden of the pub.

But this was not the last that Reynard had seen of his lover's dead husband. His ghost was to plague him and call out: 'Oh Ralph, Oh Ralph, repent, vengeance is at hand.' At Topcliffe Fair the ghost accosted Reynard, who rode home at a furious pace. The ghost preceded him, taunting him and, on approaching the White House, vanished into the grave the three had buried Fletcher in. Reynard, now out of his mind with terror, confessed the murder to his sister who called in the local magistrate. The three were tried and hung at York in 1623. But the ghost remained for many years, and coachmen noted their horses shying and showing fear when approaching the White House.

The Blue Bell's reputation came from a formidable landlady, Anne Harrison, known to all as 'Nana Ran Dan', who kept the house during much of the early part of the eighteenth century. When she died a remarkable epitaph was composed by one of her many admirers:

'Anne Harrison
Well known by the name of
Nana Ran Dan
Who was chaste but no prude
and tho' fee yet no harlot
by principle Virtuous
by Education a protestant
her freedom made her Lyable
to censure whilst her extensive
Charity made her esteemed
Her tongue and her hands were
ungovernable, but the rest of her
members she kept in subjection.
After a life of 80 years thus
Spent she died Novr. 15th 1745
Passenger
Weigh her virtues be charitable
and speak well of her'

During the coaching era the Rose and Crown was the head inn, dealing mainly with posting business. Tommy Hutchinson was a renowned postboy who worked from there, and in one day he rode to York and back five times, a total of 130 miles. Later it became a boarding and finishing school for young ladies.

The Station Hotel was built in 1892 as part of the terminus for the Easingwold railway, although the line is long closed. This was one of the smallest railway systems in Britain — it stretched just two and a half miles to join the East Coast main line. At the other end in Alne was another Station Hotel, which changed its name when the railway closed. It is now called the Winning Post — simply because the landlord at the time bought a sign with that name on it. Three miles up the line at Tollerton is yet another Station Hotel, and whilst the railway remains the station has been closed for years.

In *The Praise of Yorkshire Ale,* Easingwold also comes in for some celebration — in particular the ale brewed by a famous alewife, Nanny Driffield:

'That they did all agree with one consent:
To Easingwold they their way would pass
With Nanny Driffield there to drink a glass:
For Bacchus having heard of her strong ale
He swore by Jupiter he would not fail
To have a merry bout if he did find
Her Nappy Ale to please his princely Mind.'

'Nappy' ale is strong ale, so called because it had a 'nap' or creamy head.

Coxwold is best known because Lawrence Sterne was the vicar there in the eighteenth century. It was here that he wrote much of

The Fauconberg Arms in Coxwold was familiar to Laurence Sterne.

Tristram Shandy, his famous nine volume novel in which the character of the title hardly appears. Sterne lived opposite the Fauconberg Arms, a delightfully unspoilt seventeenth century inn named after the Earl of Fauconberg, who lived nearby and married Oliver Cromwell's daughter.

Kilburn — like Coxwold — nestles under the Hambleton Hills, and has the massive chalk-cut White Horse to overlook it. It also had its famous son, Robert Thompson the woodcarver, whose 'mouse' trademark can be found on furniture all over the world. Next to his workshop is the Foresters Arms, an eighteenth century stone-built inn. Kilburn had a medieval feast which lasted for four days and included races, quoits and a parade in which the 'Lord Mayor' and 'Lady Mayoress' of the village — in reality two young men dressed up — walked to the pub accompanied by most of the villagers.

The Fairfax Arms at Gilling East claims Cromwell as one of its former customers. Lord Fairfax was the Parliamentary general who saved York Minster from destruction in the siege of 1644. He lived at Gilling Castle and entertained the Roundhead leader in the pub. It carries a huge hop vine over the door as part of its insignia.

In Oswaldkirk the Malt Shovel was built in 1610 as a manor house, was licensed some seventy years later, and took on the role of a coaching inn in the late eighteenth century. It has some superb features, including a box maze in the rear garden.

The oldest surviving inn in Helmsley is the Crown, which dates from at least 1637 and may have origins in the middle of the sixteenth century. The present building dates from the turn of the eighteenth and nineteenth centuries, although the exterior is modern. It was once called Coopers Posting House and the inside is a delight of small rooms and passages.

The Feathers is named after a family rather than its usual source of the emblematic three feathers of the Black Prince. It was built in 1782 as a doctor's house and surgery, and in its time has served as a market toll house and ale house. The town had a Board Inn which changed its name in 1855 to the Feversham Arms when it was rebuilt by the Earl of Feversham.

The poet William Wordsworth and his sister Dorothy visited Helmsley in July 1802. Dorothy recorded in her journal:

'...slept at a very nice inn and were well treated — bright bellows and floors as smooth as ice.'

And on their return journey:

'...we stopped at the same inn where we had slept before. My heart danced at the sight of its cleanly outside, bright yellow walls, casements overshadowed with jasmine, and its low double gavel-ended front.'

The pub they stayed at was the Black Swan in the market place, parts of which are more than 400 years old. The Tudor doorway to the cellars came from the sixteenth century wing of Helmsley Castle. Estate rent days and rent dinners were held here — the pewter plates the tenants dined on are still retained and displayed. It was a coaching inn and the Helmsley Highflyer from Leeds through York to Kirkbymoorside was serviced from here. It continued until 1871 when the railway reached the town.

The Wordsworths were to return later in 1802 after William had married Mary Hutchinson on the 4th October at Brompton-by-Sawdon near Scarborough. After the wedding the three of them travelled back to the family home in the Lake District. They stopped overnight and Dorothy noted that they '...came to the comfortable inn once more'.

'My heart danced at the sight of its cleanly outside...', wrote Dorothy Wordsworth of the Black Swan at Helmsley.

In a village that features several cruck-framed buildings, the Star at Harome comes as no real surprise. Way back in the fourteenth century this inn was three cottages, but now it is one of the last remaining pubs of this form of construction in the county. It retains its open fires, wooden settles and thatched roof, and the oak-beamed bar has some 'Mousey' Thompson furnishings.

Ironworking is still a living craft at Kirkbymoorside and examples can be found in some of the market town pubs. The Black Swan became an inn in 1632 after conversion from two cruck-framed houses and retains some adzed oak beams. The Sinnington Hunt, the oldest in Britain, meets here. The George and Dragon is said to be thirteenth century; it is certainly very old and was a coaching inn with links to Leeds. They brewed their own beer here, and the brewhouse remains.

One would have expected the Sinnington Hunt to have met at Sinnington itself. At one time it did, and what was the Shoulder of Mutton there changed its name to the Fox and Hounds. The origins of the pub are in the sixteenth century.

The Grey Horse Inn at Great Edstone is a listed building of great age with an unusual carved bar and, it is said, its own ghost. And the Sun Inn at Normanby is the last remaining one of several seventeenth century alehouses in the village; it was formerly owned by Russells of Malton and was in the hands of one family for more than 100 years.

Pickering opens the gate to the moors by road and by a preserved railway. When the line opened in 1836, 7,000 people gathered for the occasion and to watch the 300 dignitaries enter the Black Swan Hotel for the celebratory feast. The landlord of the day was a shareholder, so he was presumably the first to show a profit! The inn is seventeenth century and before the railway came it serviced the coaches.

The Rose Inn also dates from the seventeenth century although it was substantially altered around 1800. Its position besides the town beck led to it being regularly flooded by up to six feet. One enterprising landlord would tell his guests to remain in their rooms and he would bring them their meals by boat and serve them through the bedroom windows. On one occasion, barrels of beer which floated away were rescued by the local police.

The Bay Horse was also a coaching inn and had its own brewhouse until 1813. Cromwell's officers were billeted here and there is still a hideaway cupboard. The uniquely-titled Lettered Board with its interesting sign is an eighteenth century town house opposite an area where the cattle market stood. Another market pub, the Forest and Vale, is Georgian with a name that reflects the ancient and continuing position of the town.

Thornton-le-Dale is often described as one of Yorkshire's 'chocolate box' villages, with its delightful old cottages and stream running alongside the main street. The Buck Hotel fits into the picture, dating from 1600, with a mounting block and stables as reminders of its coaching period. So does the New Inn, which is almost as old as the Buck; it was opened in 1607 as a post house and converted to an inn in 1740. Manor courts were held here and the stocks which are located opposite were last used in 1874.

Great Barugh, the locals will tell you, is pronounced 'Great Barf'. There, in the Golden Lion, Royalists were harboured during the Civil War. In the eighteenth century Grapes Inn at nearby Great Habton, racehorses have been housed over the years, including such prolific chasers as Night Nurse and Sea Pigeon. At Swinton the Blacksmiths Arms has a direct connection with its roots, for the present building was originally a farm, two cottages and a smithy. Parts of it are 300 years old, with walls three feet thick.

Practically every inn and pub in Malton has some interest and most are at least a century old — many are two or three. The Cross Keys in Wheelgate can claim to be an inn of sorts as far back as the twelfth century, when it was one of three hostels served by the Gilbertine canons of Malton Priory for the use of pilgrims, travellers and the homeless. Later, as an inn, it was run by the canons of St Mary's. The oldest existing part is the Gothic vaulted cellar which was the original crypt. (There was said to be a tunnel to the priory.) The sign is probably taken from the papal arms but may well be later, in which case it probably identifies with the Archdiocese of York.

The Spotted Cow in Spitalgate has been a pub since 1864 when it opened to serve the new cattle market but, as a building, it is much older. It is a listed building and is described as a '...typical, unpretentious public house building of its date'. The Crown Hotel in Wheelgate has a subtitle on its sign of 'Suddabys', relating to the family that has owned it for many years.

Malton had a great reputation as a brewing town and its coat of arms includes three casks to denote the town's three breweries: Wrangham, Russell and Rose. They are all, sadly, gone but behind the Crown is a new 'micro-brewery' built in what were once the stables. Malton has also long been a racing town — and remains so today. Some racehorses were kept at the Crown, including Double Chance which won the 1925 Grand National and after which the new Malton Brewing Company's bitter was named.

The Spitalbeck at Flaxton on the main road from Malton to York is a mile away from the beck. It was an early stagecoach house, but when the owners decided to rebuild they found a more suitable spot and retained the name.

The Spitalbeck on the Malton road was rebuilt a mile away from the beck.

The Ridings boundary split Stamford Bridge, as does that of the new counties today. The Three Cups is in the North Riding and has an interesting ancient draw well within its bounds; it is twenty-three feet deep and can be seen through a porthole in the bar. And across the bounds in the East Riding, the Swordsman — once called the New Inn — and the Bay Horse are both authentic village locals dating from the eighteenth century.

COAST AND MOORLAND

'Away they drove. Adieu! said he,
To Scarbro's sweet variety:
Sweet social spot, thy genial charm
Can labour and fatigue disarm.'

Anon, *c 1800*

Bridlington manages to combine the brash with the decorous to most people's satisfaction. The seafront pubs are either modern or modernised, but in the old town can be found some unspoilt and historic inns and pubs. Ye Olde Starre Inn should really be called simply the Star Inn, but that is the way of the world; a sixteenth century inn like this deserves better. The Pack Horse is not quite as old and was a coaching inn for the runs to Scarborough and Hull. The Board Inn takes its name from the fact that it provided bed and board for visitors — no doubt it was one of many in the town.

The barbaric pastime — already mentioned — involving a dog attacking a tethered duck in a pond received a 'royal' tag, but this is not how the 300 year old Royal Dog and Duck at Flamborough got its prefix. It was added when Prince Louis of Battenberg (father of Earl Mountbatten of Burma) visited there in 1900 — long after the 'sport' was banned. A unique name for a pub can be found at Hunmanby. It is the Veterinary Arms, where a century ago a veterinary surgeon decided to sell ale to augment his living. The name followed automatically.

Filey is a more compact seaside resort than Bridlington, smaller and eclectic. The Plough had a sign which read: 'He who by the plough would thrive, Himself must either hold or drive.' Foords Hotel is an elegant listed eighteenth century building with Doric columns. Long gone from Queen Street is the Old Ship Inn, better known as 'T' Awd Ship Inn' and remembered by a panel showing an engraving of a ship. It was the haunt of smugglers and there was a hollowed-out beam there for hiding tobacco.

There was a brewery at Sherburn up to 1922. The Ridings boundary followed the River Derwent about half a mile to the north of the village and the brewery bravely called itself the East Riding Brewery. It was owned by James Kirk and the buildings are still there. The East Riding Hotel stands nearby and was the brewery tap in an estate of thirty-seven pubs, many of which were in the North Riding. The East Riding is an old pub — probably about the same age as the Pigeon Pie, a former coaching inn, which can be dated from 1800.

There were two pubs called the Cayley Arms on the road from Pickering to Scarborough, one at Allerston which is now been renamed the Fox Covert, the other at Brompton-by-Sawdon, where William Wordsworth and Mary Hutchinson were married in 1802. They were both named after Sir George Cayley, whose family were landowners in the area and lived at Brompton Hall. He designed the first aeroplane, and in 1799 engraved a design for a fixed-wing plane which is now in the Science Museum in London. He later developed a glider with a movable tail, and then added a wheeled undercarriage. The developments continued and in 1853 the first man-carrying flight in a heavier-than-air machine took place across Bromptondale. His coachman was the reluctant aviator — afterwards he resigned in protest!

The Cayley Arms at Allerston was originally called the Osbaldeston Arms after Yorkshire's most famous sporting squire, George Osbaldeston, whose estates were so vast that he was referred to as the 'Squire of All England'. His sporting prowess has never been matched. He boxed with the army champion — and beat him; he was a fine shot with both gun and pistol; one of England's half dozen best cricketers; a rowing champion; winner of many horse races and a great gambler to boot. He once shot 97 grouse with 97 shots and rode 200 miles in less than 9 hours. And he was only five feet tall!

Snainton was the last changing station for coaches on the route from Harrogate and York to Scarborough, and consequently passengers were anxious to complete their journeys. A horn was sounded as the coach left Ebberston just over a mile away and the staff at the Coachman Inn would have the horses harnessed and ready for the

George Osbaldeston, 'Squire of All England'.

final stage. It was built for the coach trade in 1776 and is now a listed building. The Derwent Hunt has met here for many years.

The last highwayman in England was caught in a first floor room at the Denison Arms in East Ayton and was hanged at nearby Spikers Hill. Needless to say this 300 hundred year old inn has a ghost.

Scarborough was founded more than ten centuries ago, although there is evidence of a Roman signal station there from the fourth century. A few pubs go back many hundreds of years, but most of the present ones date from the Victorian era. The Barn — now a thoroughly modernised pub — was born out of farm buildings that go back to the eleventh century. It is mentioned in the *Domesday Book*, has a priests' hole and a resident ghost. The Newcastle Packet has thirteenth century origins, but its name comes from the start of the import of coal from Newcastle by packet boat in 1732. It was rebuilt in 1898 and was the place where sailors waited for their boats or for storms to die away. As they waited they would carve their initials into the woodwork of the inn.

Porritts Lane is named after one of the town's shipbuilding families, and along it stands the Three Mariners which dates from around 1300. Sadly it is no longer a public house but is preserved as a museum of what medieval waterside taverns were like. It has a profusion of secret passages, concealed cupboards with panelled doors and other hiding places used by smugglers and sailors to avoid the press gang. And, of course, it is haunted. There are links here with Richard III, whose coat of arms as Duke of Gloucester is displayed in a bedroom. Amongst the many who have sought refuge and hidden here is John Paul Jones, the eighteenth century American naval adventurer who came ashore after his ship sank following a battle with the English fleet off Flamborough Head. Eventually he made his way to France and back to America.

The inn was used as a mortuary and for inquests, particularly for mariners drowned at sea. A Norwegian ship was wrecked off Scarborough, all hands were lost and their bodies washed ashore and brought to the Three Mariners. Shortly afterwards the ship's figurehead was found and erected above the inn door as a memorial to the foreign sailors. It was the carving of a rather well-endowed lady who became known as Elvira. She was said to leave her position when storms were approaching and knock on the doors of the houses of fishermen to warn them. Later the figure was sold to an American.

A similar tale is told of the inn's resident ghost. She is headless and haunts a room that is said to have had a hole in the floor through which a man could squeeze, then scramble down a rope ladder and escape along a passage to the harbour, thus avoiding the press gang or the excisemen. Why she should choose this room or why she is headless

Scarborough's history as a spa will be better told elsewhere but it does affect the style of the Victorian public houses, hotels and gin palaces, none more so than that magnificent edifice, the Grand Hotel. Dominating South Bay and much of the town, the thirteen storey building was designed by Cuthbert Brodrick (who built Leeds Town Hall). It was opened in 1867 and established Scarborough as 'the Queen of the Watering Places'.

no-one seems to know, but she is supposed to warn fishermen of impending disaster in the same way as Elvira. Perhaps the two stories have the same root. One mystery concerns two cousins setting off in the early hours for the harbour and their coble. When near the inn the headless spectre appeared through the mist. One man saw it and took the warning. The other didn't and was sceptical of his cousin's fear. He went to sea and later that day was drowned when his boat foundered in a rough squall.

A tunnel is said to connect the Three Jolly Sailors at Burniston with the beach more than a mile away. This old inn has smuggling connections but the tunnel story, told of many old inns, is just that — a story. The Falcon just outside Claughton is close by the peat diggings, rarely found these days. It has a fire which is supposed to have burned continuously for more than 300 years. The Blacksmiths Arms in the village is hard by the smithy; this eighteenth century inn with a rather odd nineteenth century addition is the headquarters of the local marrow-growing society.

There is another Blacksmiths Arms at Hartoft End, but when it served miners in the area it was called the Pick and Shovel. It was built in the sixteenth century with stone from the destruction of Rosedale Abbey, and was originally a farmhouse where the farmer was also a blacksmith. The alehouse was a eighteenth century addition.

The White Horse, which is part way up the famous one-in-three slope of Rosedale Chimney, was also a farmhouse and alehouse combined. It has been licensed since 1702 when it was built as Lane End Farm. During the ironstone mining era it was popular with the miners. In Rosedale Abbey the Milburn Arms was once called the Crown and has beginnings in the fifteenth century. It has been a favourite for years with shooting parties.

High on the moors is the Sun Inn at Bilsdale, also known as Spout House. The present pub is next door to the original one, thatched and preserved and run as a museum by the North York Moors National Park Committee. Outside is the gravestone of Bobbie Dowson, whipper-in for the Bilsdale Hunt for sixty years. When he died in 1902 his funeral was massively attended, and his friends commissioned a special stone. The local parson banned it from the graveyard and there was a dispute which lasted for twelve years. Eventually it was resolved and the stone was placed outside the pub where the kennels had been. Five generations of Ainleys have kept the Sun; every one usually called William, and by tradition the huntsman of the Bilsdale pack.

The most attractive 200 year old Blacksmiths Arms at Lastingham once had as its innkeeper the wife of the local curate. A book published in York in 1806 entitled *Anecdotes and Manners of a few Ancient and Modern Oddities* tells us that the Reverend Jeremiah Carter had a stipend of £20 a year to keep his family of thirteen children. Not only did his wife take over the licence of the Blacksmiths, but Mr Carter also entertained his parishioners by playing the fiddle. This brought the disapprobation of his archdeacon, and the worthy but impecunious curate penned an address to defend and explain his position:

'My wife keeps a public-house, and as my parish is so wide that some of my parishioners have to come from ten to fifteen miles to church, you will readily allow that some refreshment before they return must occasionally be necessary; and when can they have it more properly than when their journey is half performed?...To divert their attention from foibles over their cups, I take down my violin and play them a few tunes, which gives me an opportunity of seeing that they get no more liquor than is necessary for refreshment; and if the young people propose a dance I seldom answer in the negative... Thus my parishioners enjoy a triple advantage of being instructed, fed, and amused at the same time.'

The address was longwinded but convincing and he concluded with an appeal to the duty of cheerfulness. The archdeacon accepted the logic of Mr Carter's case and nothing more was said. The Blacksmiths Arms today retains pleasant reminders of its past with low beams, open hearths and a cast-iron range.

Mr Carter was not the only cleric to keep an alehouse or to risk the ire of his superiors. In 1630 a number of priests and rectors were summoned before the High Commission at York for the sin of 'selling ale and beer'. It was claimed in their defence that it resulted from poverty due to low stipends (further indications were given of clerics teaching, farming and doing general labouring work).

At Hutton le Hole there is a cottage with an inscription:

'By hammer and hand all arts do stand'.

It was built in 1784, and for many years was the Hammer and Hand Inn serving the lead miners of the area, but is now a cottage again.

The Lion on Blakey Ridge is the highest inn on the North York Moors, at 1,325 feet above sea level. It is also very old, with its most authentic claim of 1552, but there is a strongly held view that it was established as a house of refreshment — and that meant ale! — by the monks of Guisborough in the fourteenth century. Innkeepers have by tradition had the right to dig for coal and retain peat cutting and pasturage rights. Nearby is a Bronze Age burial mound, and when the centre collapsed it was used as a cock pit. The Lion is on the Lyke Wake Walk route and sheep sales are held here in the autumn.

Goathland still preserves an ancient tradition in the sword dance called the 'Plough Stots', performed outside the Goathland Hotel which services the railway. The Mallyan Spout, a Victorian pub, takes its unusual name from a waterfall close by. At nearby Beck Hole, the Birch Hall Inn had a sign painted by Algernon Newton RA; he lived in the village at the former Lord Nelson Inn, which he converted into a country cottage.

A fire burned at the Wagon and Horses at Saltersgate for 170 years. The inn was built in 1650 and the fire was lit by the first landlord; it was said to keep in the spirit of a witch buried below it. This inn was a centre for smuggling, and in the mid-eighteenth century the Salt Road (sometimes called the Fish Road) was built as a link to Robin Hoods Bay. Salt was heavily taxed and was sold off here. Tea was another much sought-after commodity and three quarters of the amount consumed in Britain about that time was smuggled. In Holland it cost sevenpence a pound and was selling here, after tax, for twenty-four shillings. The cellars were used for drying and salting fish, with the salt kept in boxes in the kitchen. (It was from this that the area got its name.) Silks were another smuggled item — as was gin, carried by women in pigs' bladders under their petticoats. It was the perfect inland hiding place and was used by gangs from along the North Yorkshire coast.

Ravenscar, with some of the finest and highest cliffs in England, is at the end of the Lyke Wake Walk. There was a Roman signal station here, and the Raven Hall Hotel was built on the site of it in 1774. It was said to have been a retreat for George III during his insane periods. In 1826, the King's physician, Doctor Willis, came to live here and rebuilt it. There are terraced gardens on the edge of the cliffs and the hotel has a detached coach house.

Robin Hoods Bay — or Bay Town — has a public house with the distinction of being the only one against which a ship has been wrecked. It happened in 1893 when the brig Romulus was smashed by high tides against the Bay Hotel and its mast came through the main bar window. The hotel was built in 1843 after a high tide had washed away its predecessor. During the great storms along the East Coast in 1953 it was surrounded by water. On the original building there was a platform on the sea side to haul goods from boats at high tide. The Court Leet of Fylingdales continues to be held here every December, although what was a medieval court of record has no powers today.

The town was a hotbed of smuggling, and there were several underground passages linking inns with houses. In 1822 a coastguard station was established here with the main object of preventing contraband entering the country. The crew of a lugger narrowly escaped capture by using one of the tunnels from the Nags Head, and others took their freedom through a culverted beck to the sea. A favourite tale is of the cargo of brandy siezed at the Fishermans Arms. The excisemen opened it, tasted it to check its authenticity, became drunk and their prisoners escaped!

The Fishermans Arms was built in 1680 and later became the Kings Arms, but is now the men's institute.

One of Whitby's many historians wrote in 1817 of it being '...furnished with no less than 48 inns, coffee houses and public houses, some of which are very ancient'.

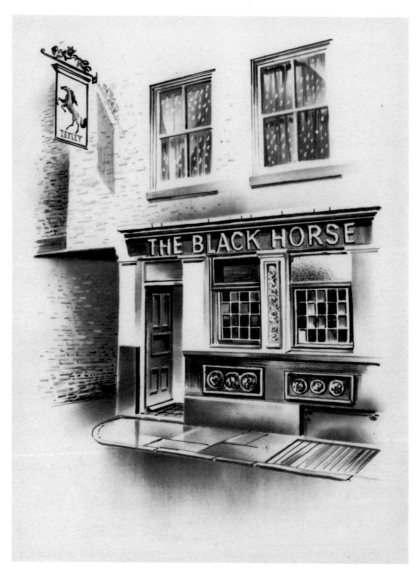

The Black Horse is the oldest trading pub in the town and its yard was once the midden of St Hilda's Monastery. When the pub was rebuilt in 1874, bones, shells and domestic waste were found here. This was a smuggler's inn, though later legitimised when it serviced the coaching trade, and is now the haunt of fishermen.

The Old Ship Launch, which later became the Old Smuggler Cafe, had a sign which proclaimed it 'The home of the Press Gang', and it was said that those who consumed too much there would be 'encouraged' to join the navy. To some extent it carried this task forward when during the Great War it displayed recruiting posters. The first name came from the shipyard just behind and it was the favourite of the shipbuilders. Naturally it had smuggling connections and was another inn with a secret passage to the harbour.

There is a great literary tradition in Whitby. The Victorian writer Elizabeth Gaskell set her novel *Sylvia's Lovers* in Whitby, thinly disguised as 'Monkshaven'. She also renamed the inn in the story where the press gang had its headquarters as the Mariners Arms. Bram Stoker visited and set his masterpiece *Dracula* here but there is no record in fact or fiction that either author or leading character drank in the town. But in 1844 Charles Dickens stayed at the White Horse and Griffin, previously a favourite of Captain James Cook. The novelist Wilkie Collins wrote to Dickens from Whitby saying that the inn was up a back yard with no view from the best room.

The seventeenth century Golden Lion stands next to the Customs House and was the location of the first masonic lodge in the town in 1764. The Little Angel is on the site of the brewhouse of an abbey, possibly twelfth century, although the present building dates from 1823. There is a medieval casement inside and on the outer wall is a boundary post marking the parishes of Whitby and Ruswarp.

In the eighteenth century the White Horse in Church Street was an important meeting place for the gentlemen of the town and sea captains. Coaches ran from here twice weekly to York, the cost being fourteen shillings inside and eight shillings outside. The Angel played its part in railway history when a share list was displayed there in 1832 to promote the railway between Whitby and Pickering planned by George Stephenson. He met here with George Hudson, the 'Railway King', in 1834 and the line opened two years later.

Egton Bridge has been the home of a gooseberry show every August since 1800. It was also the home of Father Nicholas Postgate, the last of the English martyrs who was hanged at York in 1679. The Postgate is built on the site of the priest's house.

The Horseshoe Hotel is a nineteenth century country house in its own grounds by the River Esk. It may well take its name from the implements in a game of quoits which is a popular sport in in Eskdale. It is similar to the American game of tossing horseshoes, but quoits are rings of steel thrown to a hob in a bed of clay. The sport was first mentioned in 1365 and was once made illegal by Richard II.

The Fox and Hounds at Ainthorpe dates from 1555 and retains a stone fireplace taken from Danby Castle, the home of Catherine Parr, the sixth and final wife of Henry VIII. Cromwell is said to have slept at the pub, and J B Priestley certainly did; he may well have used it as the pattern for his play *I Have Been Here Before.*

In West Eskdale at Castleton, at a meeting of moorland roads, the Robin Hood and Little John used to display the welcoming sign:

'Kind Gentlemen and Yeoman good,
Call in and drink with Robin Hood.
If Robin Hood be not at home,
Step in and drink with Little John.'

The Royal George in Staithes is an ancient village pub and is a listed building. The original Cod and Lobster was probably built in the sixteenth century but it has been washed away three times, including as recently as 1953 when the kitchen, scullery and two bedrooms were completely destroyed and the entire bottle stock was washed out to sea. For months trade continued in a small room until rebuilding took place. Now the walls are more than a foot thick with steel rods inside them.

At the busy junction where roads link Yarm, Thirsk and Stokesley, the Cleveland Tontine Inn has stood since 1804 following the building of the turnpike between Thirsk and Yarm (now the A19 trunk road). It arose in similar circumstances to the Tontine in Sheffield, which preceded it by twenty years. 100 shares of £25 were raised, and later a further twenty additional ones came on the market to provide extra stabling. The original proposal was that when the shareholders were reduced to three the property would become theirs in proportion to the number of shares held.

But as the Cleveland Tontine was essentially a coaching inn linking Newcastle and Sunderland with the Yorkshire cities and as far as London, it fell from grace with the coming of the railways. The licence was transferred to a smaller inn, which did not succeed, and by the turn of the century it had become a private house. Today, happily, it is back in business again as a inn catering for the demands of modern travel.

Jet was mined on the Cleveland moors and along the coast in great quantities in the nineteenth century. In its heyday around 1870 more than 200 men were working in the mines. They are remembered by the Jet Miners Arms at Great Broughton (although its origins are in 1750 before jet mining began). The jet was sold and taken to Whitby where some 1,500 people were employed in the skilled carving and selling of jewellery and ornaments.

The Ship Inn at Saltburn probably dates from the sixteenth or seventeenth century when it was an undeveloped fishing village. John Andrews was once the landlord there and he combined the incongruous occupations of innkeeper, master of the Roxby Hunt and leader of a gang of smugglers. He went to jail twice and died there in 1835. The Zetland Hotel is the oldest railway hotel in the world. Building started there in 1860 and it opened in 1863 with its own platform to allow guests to enter the hotel under cover.

The Wharton Arms at Skelton is another pub with the unlikely tale of a passage that led to the coast. As this is nearly two miles away it seems neither feasible nor logical. But it was certainly a centre for smuggling, and quantities of lace and brandy passed through here with the contrabandmen. It continues to carry the nickname of 'Skippers'.

Middlesborough, on the south bank of the Tees, now labours under being part of the county of Cleveland. It is a new town with its first origins no later than 1830, as a song written in 1902 by Elizabeth Normington proclaims:

'Prosperous Middlesbro', Industrious Middlesbro',
The new town of Middlesbro', the Pride of the Tees.'

This prosperity and industry was responsible for a rapid increase in the number of public houses and beerhouses during Victoria's days, but this leaves us today with little by way of historical relics either in bricks and mortar or anecdotes. It seems the first pub was opened in 1830 and appropriately it was called the King William IV after the reigning monarch. Inevitably it became known as the 'King Billy.'

Other early pubs which have survived include the Ship Inn, first licensed in 1831 and one of the few remaining links with the original 'new' town. The Middlesborough Hotel was built in 1846 on the site of the old Middlesborough farm, which had predated the town by many years. It later became a shop and was demolished in 1963. As in many other Yorkshire towns, sport often had its roots in the town's public houses; at the Talbot in South Street a meeting was held in 1876 at which Middlesborough Football Club was formed.

But this new town was not slow to react against the 'demon drink', and the Middlesborough Temperance Society was formed there as

The historic George and Dragon in Yarm — next door to the Union Arms — has a place in the nation's economic history.

early as 1834. Later the society organised gigantic garden parties, days out and sea excursions, and was responsible for persuading a local benefactor to make the gift of a public park in which: 'No intoxicating beverages of any kind shall be sold or vended within the boundaries of the said park by any person or persons whatsoever.'

The historic George and Dragon in Yarm has its place in the nation's economic and industrial history. It was here that the first meeting of the promoters of the Stockton and Darlington Railway was held, and a bronze plaque on the wall of the pub commemorates this:

'In the Commercial Room of this hotel on the 12th day of February, 1820 was held the Promoters' Meeting of the Stockton and Darlington Railway — the first public railway in the world. Thomas Meynell, Esq., of Yarm presided.'

The room in which the meeting was held is still preserved to this day. There are memories, too, of its earlier period as a coaching inn, with ticket boxes and recesses for gentlemens' wigs for when their owners refreshed themselves. Its neighbour the Union Arms dates from 1762 and retains its coaching arch to the yard.

Yarm had sixteen inns in 1848 and the oldest, the Ketton Ox, goes back more than 400 years. It takes its name from a famous shorthorn bred by Charles Colling of Ketton which weighed 220 stone. In 1801 he was offered £2,000 for it and refused. There are two rooms on the top floor and one of them was the official cockpit until it was declared illegal in 1849. The other then became the unofficial venue, and had such facilities as a set of secret stairs to the floor below and a chute which the cocks were sent down to a shed in the yard.

On the high street a house still displays a sign for the Tom Brown Inn, although it is many years since it closed. It commemorates Trooper Tom Brown of Blands Dragoons who, at the Battle of Dettingen in 1743, distinguished himself by recovering the regimental standard after it had been taken by the enemy. He retired to Yarm with a pension of £30 a year and they named a pub after him.

THE DALES

Piercebridge straddles the Tees, and while most of the village is in County Durham its most famous inn, the George, is on the Yorkshire side of the river. In the bar of this seventeenth century coaching inn is the original clock that inspired a famous music hall song. It was craftsman-made in Darlington for two brothers who kept the George. It had perfect timing, but when one of the brothers died the works went awry; however it continued working. When the second brother, who lived to be eighty, passed away, the clock stopped and it was impossible to make it work again. It attracted the attention of Henry Clay Work, a one-time customer there, and by the late 1870's his song was the rage of London:

> 'My grandfather's clock was too large for the shelf
> So it stood ninety years on the floor.
> It was taller by half than the old man himself
> Though it weighed not a pennyweight more.'

— and so it goes through his life:

> 'Tick-tock, tick-tock, his life-seconds numbering...'

— until he goes to join the choir invisible, and then:

> 'But it stopped short — never to go again —
> When the old man died.'

Work was an American who also wrote the words for the temperance song which featured another clock:

> 'Father, dear father, come home with me now,
> The clock in the steeple strikes one.'

Charles Dickens travelled four times to Yorkshire, but the visit most remembered was that in 1838 to Greta Bridge and the Bowes area in search of information for his forthcoming book *Nicholas Nickleby,* which appeared later that year in monthly parts.

Dickens' predeliction for inns came out in both his writings and in reports of his life. He was known to be a expert in wine and his home at Gads Hill contained a large cellar. Some of the pubs from Dickens' novels are well known: the Great White Horse at Ipswich and the George and Vulture, both from *Pickwick's Papers,* and the Saracens Head in Snow Hill, London, where Nickleby set out on his journey to Yorkshire. Amongst some other inns Dickens visited in Yorkshire were the New Angel at Doncaster, the George in Bradford and the White Horse and Griffin in Whitby.

Greta Bridge was the second night's stop for coaches on the London to Carlisle route. Dickens and his friend Hablot K Browne — 'Phiz' the cartoonist — arrived there on a freezing, snowblind night in January 1838. He was later to refer to what was then called the New Inn as '...the best inn I have ever put up at', but it was not his first impression, as he wrote to his wife:

'...We have driven through snow from Grantham, paid £6 for two places inside...arrived 11 pm, we reached a bare place with a house standing alone in the midst of a dreary moor, which the guard informed us was Greta Bridge...it was fearfully cold, and there was no outward signs of anyone being up in the house. But to our great joy we discovered a comfortable room with drawn curtains and a most blazing fire...in half an hour, they gave us a smoking supper and a bottle of mulled port...then we retired to a couple of capital bedrooms, in each of which there was a roaring fire halfway up the chimney.'

He went to describe their most fulsome breakfast:

'...toast, cakes, a Yorkshire pie, a piece of beef about the size and much the shape of my portmanteau, tea, coffee, ham and eggs.'

When the journey was repeated in the novel, things were a little different. Nickleby stayed outside the 'George and New Inn' and noted that Wackford Squeers, his new master, had gone inside to 'stretch his legs'. He continued:

'After some minutes he returned with his legs thoroughly stretched, if the hue of his nose and a short hiccup afforded any criterion.'

This variously named inn — which has the Morritt Arms as its successor — had other famous visitors, including Walter Scott whose epic poem *Rokeby* is titled after the nearby estate; Scott was a friend of the Squire of Rokeby. Another visitor was the artist J M W Turner, who had a great love for the Yorkshire landscape.

Dickens journeyed from Greta Bridge to the Unicorn at Bowes, the town where he found the model for Dotheboys Hall and where it is thought he wrote part of *Nicholas Nickleby*. It was originally called the George and was an important coaching inn on the road from the Great North Road across the Pennines to Brough and Penrith. A former landlord, John Railton, brought financial ruin upon himself by improving the road over Stainmore, a consequence of which was that eastbound coaches then pushed on to Greta Bridge before changing horses instead of stopping at his inn. The railway brought more bad times, but the motor car spelt rejuvenation and the inn flourishes today.

Croft was first noticed as a spa in the later seventeenth century and its first posting house was built in 1704. It is said the waters were also

Lord Byron's honeymoon was spent at the Croft Spa Hotel

good for horses — both for drinking and paddling. The Croft Spa Hotel was built in Georgian times and in its heyday had a ballroom with a musicians' gallery and a grand dining room. Lewis Carroll's father was the Rector of St Peters at Croft and the author spent his boyhood here. And the honeymoon of Lord Byron's shortlived marriage was spent at the Spa Hotel. Croft declined as a spa as Harrogate thrived, and although there was a revival around 1914 the baths and spa are closed.

The Bridge House Hotel at Catterick originated in the fifteenth century, probably when the bridge over the Swale was built in 1422. A lease of 1535 shows it as the Bridge Inn, although it later became the George when Daniel Ferguson was the landlord. He stayed for forty years during the great coaching days and his initials are cut in the stone of the lounge windows. He loved sport and cockfighting was his great passion; he organised mains at the Salutation Inn of fifty-one cocks with betting of £5 on each fight and £50 on the main.

His coaching business was big and he often had to command plough and dray horses to work the coaches. There were some customers who would demand only the best, one of these being the Duke of Cleveland who would order the postboys to 'drive like the devil'. Mr Ferguson would listen to this and exhort the lads to '...attend to his Grace's orders...', and then under his breath, '...but don't overboil the eggs'.

The Angel and the Golden Lion — now closed — were also coaching inns but not as important as the George. The Angel had stabling for 100 horses, but was mainly used as a stud for racehorses and coach horses and was a favourite with racegoers. It is haunted by a nun who was imprisoned beneath the church for being over-familiar with the local priest. Naturally there is a tunnel between the inn and the church.

Horseracing has played a big part in the economy of the area and several inns have associations through their names. The Beeswing at East Cowton recalls one of the most successful horses of the mid-nineteenth century, and the Voltigeur at Barton takes the name of the 1850 Derby winner which is also remembered by one of the big races at York, the Great Voltigeur Stakes. At Crakehall near Bedale the Bay

Catterick's Angel was a favourite with racegoers.

Horse was previously called the Octavian, and there is a pub called the Revellers at Yafforth near Northallerton. Both these horses won the St Leger at Doncaster.

There is no longer an inn called the Lass of Richmond Hill in the Yorkshire town (although, incongruously, one remains in Surrey), but the famous song dedicated to Frances I'Anson belongs to Yorkshire. The Bishop Blaize in the market place is an early eighteenth century building which has a roof of stone slates pegged with sheep bones. Bishop Blaize is the patron saint of woolcombers, and in medieval days the town had a thriving wool industry.

The Turf Tavern is in a group of buildings that includes the famous Georgian Theatre and was named for the defunct Richmond racecourse. The Black Lion may well have seventeenth century origins but some guides claim the Bishop Blaize as the oldest surviving inn. The eighteenth century Kings Head Hotel has eight bays and was one of the town's principal coaching inns.

Outside the town the stone-built Holly Hill stands next to an old toll house on the Newcastle to Lancaster turnpike, but this is now only a minor road leading to Hipswell Moor. The latter is where the Halfpenny House used to stand. The name was a corruption of Halfway House but came about because an illegal toll of a halfpenny was levied. Even after the authorities clamped down the toll continued, and was paid over to Richmond Hospital. The Bay Horse at Tunstall was built as a village alehouse in 1760 and continues that function to this day. At one time it was about to be moved stone by stone to a folk museum in York, but happily it was given a reprieve.

The Tan Hill Inn is the highest in England at 1,732 feet above sea level. It was built in 1737 and was once known as the Kings Pit after one of the many coal mines in the area. Its original purpose was to serve the miners who worked there, as well as the drovers and pack horse traders. Its remoteness and elevation have led to it being snowed up and isolated for many weeks at a time. The story goes that one year a former landlord wished a shepherd friend of his a 'Happy New Year' on the 16th April!

The Tan Hill Inn — the highest in England — used to serve the coal miners who worked nearby.

It stands at a crossroads on the Durham border where once there was a toll house. For a period, insensitive legislation took it out of Yorkshire but demand has brought it back. No-one lives within five miles of Tan Hill, and with the decline of mining before the Great War the licence lapsed for a while; but it reopened to service travellers — those on foot in particular, for it stands on the Pennine Way. Shepherds and farmers are also amongst its customers, and they turn up in their hundreds for the Swaledale Sheep Fair — the Tan Hill Show — in May of each year. Its most famous and best-loved licensee was Susan Peacock, who was there for thirty-five years. Her husband was the last of the area's coal miners, extracting the fuel single-handedly for the inn fire. She is remembered by a slab of rock behind the pub:

'IN MEMORY OF
SUSAN PEACOCK
WHO DIED 24 MAY 1937
LIVED HERE FROM 1902'

Among the many anecdotes of her is her description of a day on which the wind was so strong she said it '...would blow the horns off a tup'.

There was another remote inn, the Cat Hole at Keld, which Denzil Batchelor in his *The English Inn* calls '...the loneliest inn in the world'. Another description says it is the '...last outpost of civilisation before the traveller sets out to cross the Pennines'. On down Arkengarthdale is the CB, which may well be the nearest building to the Tan Hill Inn. CB recalls Sir Charles Bathhurst, owner of most of the lead mines in the area. He developed the industry here in the early seventeenth century and every pig of lead produced had his initials on. The CB, which vies for the shortest pub name in England, dates from around 1750.

There were once shops on the ground floor of what is now the Black Bull at Reeth. It is 300 years old and a listed building that formerly served the coaching trade. At Long Row the Punch Bowl is more than 350 years old and has been frequented by the author and vet, James Herriot, since the 1930's. The Farmers Arms at Muker is a genuine farmers' local. It is the focal point of the village and was once kept by 'Old Nanny Peacock', a famous 'Swardill' character who was no doubt related to the Tan Hill's most celebrated licensee.

There are more remote inns in Dentdale and Garsdale. The 250 year old Sun at Dent recalls an enigmatic sign that read: 'Best Ale Under the Sun.' Those persistent travellers the Wordsworths visited the Garsdale Hall, and Dorothy recorded: 'We noted well the public-house where we baited, and drunk our pint of ale.' William Wordsworth and his sister were also nearby at Hardraw to see the falls and, like today, had to pass through the Green Dragon to reach what, at 100 feet, is the longest unbroken fall in England. They were here in 1802 and Wordsworth wrote about it to his friend Coleridge:

'We soon reached an inn at a place called Hardraw...after warming ourselves by the cottage fire we walked up the brookside to take a view [of the falls]. We were disappointed in the cascade though the introductory and accompanying banks were a noble mixture of grandeur and beauty. We walked up to the fall and what would I not give if I could convey to you the images and feelings which were then communicated to me.'

A more recent tale concerns the disingenuous American who said to a local: 'An awful lot of water must go over there'. This received the typical Tyke reply: 'Well it will do, there's nowt to stop it.'

A tradition of blowing the forest horn continues at the Rose and Crown in Bainbridge, an inn which was once a row of cottages on the village green of this delightful Wensleydale village. It is a tradition that dates from the thirteenth century when this was forest, and three long notes sounded out every night between Holyrood Day in September and Shrovetide to recall wanderers and shepherds. The original horn is now at Bolton Castle but the present one is hung in the passageway of the inn during the period it is in use. It says 1445 over the porch, which may be an accurate date of the life of the building. It is recorded in the parish register that in 1500 '...the housewives of Bainbridge were tippling on the Sabbath at the Rose and Crown instead of attending Divine Service.'

One of the great characters in Wensleydale — and there have been many — lived in what is now the Kings Arms at Askrigg. John Pratt built it as a private manor house and stables in 1767 and lived there until his death in 1785. He was a great racing man who started life as a jockey at Newmarket. He owned the filly Imperatrix which won the St Leger in 1782, and he was successful as a breeder of racehorses (although he made a bad error of judgement in selling one horse for 700 guineas which was immediately sold on to the Prince of Wales for 2,000 guineas). Another of his horses, Mare Phoenix, gave its name to an inn in Askrigg. After his death he was described in a punning epitaph as:

'A character so excentric, so varible, so valuable,
Astonish'd the Age he liv'd in.
Tho' small his Patrimony,
Yet, assisted by that, and his own Genius,
He, for upwards of thirty years,
Supported all the Hospitality
Of an ancient Baron.'

Joseph Lodge converted part of the house into the Kings Arms in 1800 to service the recently-completed turnpike from Darlington through Richmond to Lancaster (it had a toll office in Askrigg market square). It was the headquarters of the Equitable, Benevolent and Friendly Society which Mr Lodge formed in 1809. For many years afterwards the members held their annual meeting on the first Thursday in June, when they would march in procession through the town, attend church service and then dine together at the Kings Arms. In more recent days it has appeared as the 'Drovers Inn' in the television programme *All Creatures Great and Small*.

The Dales seem to be the place for uniquely-named inns, and nowhere else in the world will you find one called the Palmer Flatt Hotel. It is close to the beautiful falls at Aysgarth. The name comes from the practice of pilgrims returning from the Holy Land during the crusades bearing palms and seeking sanctuary at the hospice that was on the present site — they were known as 'palmers'. Coincidentally the other inn in the village is called the George and Dragon; the name celebrates the allegorical triumph of Christianity over evil after St

George, the patron saint of England, was said to have come to aid of crusaders at Antioch in 1098.

In the delightful village of West Burton (which guide books tend to describe as being 'the entrance to Bishopdale' but which I prefer to call 'the foot of Waldendale') the Fox and Hounds presides over the impressive village green. It was built around 1600 alongside a packhorse trail that led over Buckden Pike into upper Wharfedale, and it is said that the ghost of an ancient drover can be seen around the pub.

One of the surprising things about Dales history is discovering how much industry not associated with rural areas went on there at one time. West Witton was a leadmining town, although extraction ceased in the middle of the nineteenth century. The Wensleydale Heiffer would have seen it all, for it dates from the seventeenth century. The Fox and Hounds stretches back even further, as it was once a monk's house attached to Jervaulx Abbey; it is said to be the oldest building in West Witton, dating from around 1400. A fifteenth century inglenook fireplace was uncovered here during recent alterations. Leyburn's fine sloping market square is sur-rounded by inns, including the outstanding Golden Lion, a seven-teenth century coaching house. It was called Fothergills until 1885 after the presiding family. In recent years it has revived the tradition of home brewing, and the impressive bitter beer is named 'Oliver John' after the landlord's son.

East Witton was wiped out by the plague in 1563 but rebuilt as a model village in 1809. The Blue Lion dates from then and is next to the Blue Lion Stables. This unusual name may have some connection with Denmark, for such an animal can be found on that country's royal arms. The nearby Cover Bridge Inn dates from the fifteenth century, probably from the time the original bridge was built; and the Foresters Arms at Carlton-in-Coverdale, which is 450 years old, retains a table from Coverham Abbey even older than the inn.

The wide market place of Bedale contains all its inns but one, and that is the oldest. The Oddfellows Arms in Emgate was built in the sixteenth century, but its name is from later when it was the meeting

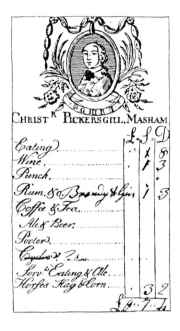

The Black Bull in Paradise is where
    Theakstons first brewed.

A bill from the Kings Head,
    Masham, in 1792.

place of the Independent Order of Oddfellows, a benevolent society
that started life in the 1820's. It is haunted by a lady in blue. In the
market square the Kings Head is late seventeenth century but was
built in the Jacobean style.

It was in the yard of the Black Bull pub at Masham that the
Theakston family started their brewery in 1827. The pub is
remembered today by a hospitality suite at the present brewery named
the Black Bull in Paradise, as it stands in Paradise Fields. The Kings
Head is the town's most important inn, standing guard over one of
the largest market squares in Yorkshire. It was built in the middle of
the eighteenth century and was a coaching and posting house. Up to
1850 the excise office was to be found there, where taxes were collected
and licences issued. The stables remain, as does a magnificent
Georgian staircase.

The White Bear, however, despite many claims, is neither old nor does it stand next door to the brewery. It is next to the offices where brewing took place until 1919, but Theakston's present brewery is across the town. And the pub only dates from 1941 when the original on the main road was destroyed by German aircraft jettisoning bombs after a raid on Teesside.

No-one born in Yorkshire has lived longer than Henry Jenkins. He was born at Ellerton-on-Swale in 1501 and died at Bolton-on-Swale, where he is buried in the graveyard, in 1670 at the age of 169. He is best remembered by the Henry Jenkins Inn at Kirkby Malzeard. In his days he worked as farm labourer, a butler, a thatcher and a river fisherman. When he topped the century he could still swim across the Swale. He had a predigious memory and was often called upon to give evidence in court cases. On one occasion a lawyer came to see him and approached an elderly man outside Henry's cottage — only to be referred inside to the man's father. This man then sent the attorney out the back to find his father, Henry Jenkins, chopping sticks! In 1743 the Master of Magdalene College, Cambridge, composed an elegant epitaph to Henry Jenkins which declared:

'Blush not marble, to rescue from oblivion the memory of HENRY JENKINS; a person obscure in birth, but of a life truly memorable; for he was enriched with the goods of nature, if not of fortune, and happy in the duration, if not variety, of his enjoyments...'

CRAVEN

'Amongst the mountains high
Of Craven, where blue heads for caps put on the sky.'

M Drayton

In the middle of the nineteenth century the market town of Bentham had eighteen public houses. Now there are only six, split between the twin communities of High and Lower Bentham, one of the most westerly outposts of the West Riding, just eleven miles from the Irish Sea.

One of the originals, Fourlands, was the only pub in England that did not sell draught beer, only bottled. It was a working farmhouse two miles outside the town and, being halfway to both Ingleton and Burton-in-Lonsdale, a suitable place for refreshment for folk walking between the three townships. The Frankland family kept Fourlands for more than a century, and up to it closing in 1980 it was tied to the Yates and Jackson Brewery of Lancaster. Following the breakdown of the firm's bottling plant some years before, supplies of bottled beer came from another brewery, so the Fourlands had another unique distinction of being the only tied public house that did not sell beers from its own brewery.

Another of the pubs now gone is the Kings Arms; it closed in 1866 but before that was the leading inn in the town. It became a grocer's shop and later a bank. It dated back to the sixteenth century, and a stone on the wall with the inscription 'WWM 1741' was merely an indication of when it had been refurbished. George Fox, the founder of the Society of Friends or the Quakers, was brought here in 1650 as a prisoner of Cromwell from Lancaster on his way to confinement at Scarborough Castle. He wrote in his journal:

'They hurried me away about 14 miles to Bentham, though I was very weak; I was hardly able to sit on horseback, and my clothes smelt so of smoke that they were loathsome to myself...many of the gentry of the country were come in and abundance of people to stare at me.'

He went on to say that he was allowed to rest but that they pressed on to Giggleswick where they stayed the night. Ironically in the latter days of its life the owner of the Kings Arms, Thomas Atkinson, built an assembly room which was used by some religious groups, including the Society of Friends.

One house had a somewhat chequered career, starting life as the Victoria, a hotel to serve travellers on the railway. Later it became the vicarage and then reverted back to the licensed trade as the Wenning Hotel; it then lost its licence and became a private hotel and is now offices. The Black Horse was in business from 1783 until 1859, except for a period of of four years when the owner, Christopher Knowles, refused to renew the licence. He sold it in 1850 and it was restored as an inn.

The Punch Bowl in Lower Bentham has drip stones on its front and on a barn extension, with the initials IW on both but with dates on them of 1670 and 1708 respectively, indicating that it had been extended. A mounting stone is still there, and inside is a magnificent Victorian engraved glass door panel.

The Punch Bowl's dripstone shows its age.

196

A Victorian door at the Punch Bowl.

In 1849, in the wake of a number of failing industries, the railway brought prosperity to Ingleton by opening up the area for tourists. Within twenty years, excursion trains on Bank Holidays brought more than 6,000 people a day to the town. They would visit the Wheatsheaf, once owned by Samuel Worthington, one of the founders of the Ingleton Improvement Association which opened up walkways to the falls and other attractions and charged threepence per person to use them. Rival organisations tried to provide alternatives but the association persevered. Worthington, ever anxious to increase trade, built a dance pavilion behind the hotel.

John Kidd, also a member of the improvement association, built the Ingleborough Hotel, which is now an old people's home. The association remains and is now called the Ingleton Scenery Company. The Black Bull, built in 1770, is now a shop; and the Bridge opened in 1830 to service what must have been one of the country's first bypasses. It was once the home of the public hangman.

The Marton Arms at Thornton-in-Lonsdale started life as a meeting house for the thirteenth century St Oswald's Church that stands opposite. It is dated 1679 but thought to be older, and in its time was a coaching inn called the Church Stile. The Reverend John Hutton, an intrepid traveller, visited there in 1781 to explore Yordas Cave and noted in his journal: 'I took from the Church Stile a guide, candles, lanthorn and tinder box.'

Clapham is a potholing centre and the home of the famous *Dalesman* magazine, which since 1939 has been a must for Yorkshiremen all over the world. The eighteenth century New Inn indicates by its name that there have been others in the village. The Flying Horseshoe at Clapham Station, which is a mile away from the village, is of similar age and carries the arms of the Farrer family who dominated and owned much of the area.

Chapel-le-Dale at the foot of Ingleborough is the heartland of caving country and a suitable place for tackling the famous three peaks of Yorkshire — although the official starting point is Horton-in-Ribblesdale where the seventeenth century Crown Hotel faces an ancient packhorse bridge.

The Hill Inn is the climber's inn. It was built in 1615 and amongst its many visitors were Robert Southey, the poet laureate; J M W Turner, the artist; Lord Tweedsmuir, better-known perhaps as John Buchan; and Dr Edith Summerskill, the Labour cabinet minister. In their more relaxed moments, climbers have been known to make a circuit of the bar without touching the floor!

At Grierstones on the edge of Gayle Moor there was an inn which the traveller, John Byng, recorded in a not too complimentary light:

'...a seat of misery, in a desert...my friend, who knew the house, forced his way through...and interned himself in the only wainscotted bed room upstairs, where at length we procured some boil'd slices of stale pork, and some fry'd eggs, with some wretched beer and brandy — to which my hunger was not equal; and from which my delicacy revolted.'

There has been an inn at Slaidburn since the thirteenth century, originally known as the Dog Inn and since 1875 as the Hark to

Bounty, one of several 'Hark to...' inns in Yorkshire. Squire Wrigglesworth was the master of the local hunt and Bounty was his favourite hound. When they picked up the scent of the fox, Bounty was the loudest and the squire would call out 'Hark [listen] to Bounty'. The Swainmote Court was held here to deal with offenders of the laws of the Royal Forest of Bowland, and the courtroom and jury box are still there.

Room thirteen at the Ribblesdale Arms at Guisburn is said to be haunted. (The inn was built by Thomas Lister in 1635 and it was an important coaching house.) The ghost is a girl who was seduced in the room and made pregnant by Lord Ribblesdale, 'a rake and waster'. She returns to it to seek revenge. Because of its reputation the room is not let unless the owners of the pub are implored to do so. Even then there is a bell fitted alongside the bed to ring for assistance.

The Inn at Whitewell was originally the manor house where the keeper of the King's deer park lived in the fourteenth century. It was owned by the Townsley family in the nineteenth century after Lord Townsley bought it through a trick. It was to be sold by auction and his lordship said he was coming to the sale. He appeared to be late and the auctioneer delayed the start, but a rather drunk and noisy tramp kept demanding that the sale begin. For a joke the auctioneer knocked down the property to the tramp for a much lower figure that it should have commanded, whereupon the tramp revealed himself as Lord Townsley, who insisted on the sale being honoured.

There have been alterations and extensions to the Inn at Whitewell in both the Georgian and Victorian periods, but it retains some carved stone fireplaces and original oak beams. It is now owned by the Queen in her capacity as the Duke of Lancaster.

The ghost of a former landlord who hanged himself in the cellar is said to reside at the Boars Head at Long Preston. This early eighteenth century house was originally built as stables for the local landowner, and became a pub in 1752 when it serviced coaches on the toll road. The ghost is passive and annoys no-one; an old photograph in the bar is said to be the man's mother and as long as that remains there he will not return.

The splendid market town of Settle has some fine old pubs but the most interesting is now just a cafe. Ye Olde Naked Man which stands opposite the town hall has a datestone of 1663. On the stone is a carving of a figure who is not naked and appears to be holding a kind of medieval plane (he was probably a local carpenter). On the side of a house at nearby Langcliffe is a carved stone with a figure and the lettering ISMS 1660, all that is left of the Naked Woman Inn and companion to the one in Settle.

The Black Horse in Giggleswick is said to date from 1663. One guide also claims it as a place where George Fox the Quaker was imprisoned. But if the historic records of Bentham are to be believed, he passed by and spent only one night here in 1650.

High on the watershed of Bishopdale before the drop to Wharfedale can be found the White Lion at Cray. This sturdy seventeenth century inn was used by packhorse traders and drovers, and its attractions continue to bring in travellers.

Below on the edge of Langstrothdale Chase is Hubberholme, where the church, bridge and inn make up one of the smallest conservation areas in Yorkshire. Here is the George, a mix of eighteenth and nineteenth century buildings that in their time have been farmhouse and vicarage, and until recently were owned by the ecclesiastical commissioners, the rent going to the vicar's stipend. This traditional and unspoilt inn has two stone-flagged rooms and retains some of its original mullioned windows. The village was a favourite of the author, J B Priestley, who is buried in the churchyard.

Behind the George is a sixteen acre field known as Poor Pasture, which is let off by auction on the first Monday in each New Year. It is called the 'candle auction' because its duration is determined by the burning of a candle, and is conducted at a ceremony in which the 'Lords' — the vicar, the churchwardens and the past tenant — go into one room; and the 'Commons' — the rest of the customers — go into the other. The proceeds go to the old folk of the parish.

At Buckden the eighteenth century Buck Inn stands guard over the village green, with the imposing 2,300 foot Buckden Pike as a backdrop. The sign for the Fox and Hounds at Starbotton is unusual

The George in Hubberholme was J B Priestley's favourite pub.

A case of role reversal! The sign of the Fox and Hounds at Starbotton.

in that it displays a hunt in progress with the fox on horseback in the middle of it. The pub is in the vernacular style of the Dales, and there is a datestone of 1834 with the inscription 'R & I Lodge', probably indicating the builders.

Charity often leaves its mark by way of commemorative plaques, statues and some buildings, but rarely by a public house. But at Linton-in-Craven the Fountaine Inn on the village green is named after Richard Fountaine, who endowed the almshouses which stand opposite. The inn is seventeenth century and a listed building. One of its attractions is the ancient game of 'ringing the bull', in which the contestants have to swing a ring attached by cord to the ceiling and try to hook on to a bull's horn on the wall.

What is now the Buck Inn at Malham was once a shooting lodge. It was rebuilt in 1820 by Walter Morrison MP who lived at Malham Tarn House. The mosaic on the floor of the inn was given by John Ruskin who was a friend of Morrison's. The tourist potential of Malhamdale has been exploited over the years, and quite rightly the inns and pubs have responded. The nineteenth century Lister Arms secured a stripe from the folk singer and walker Mike Harding when in his book *Walking the Dales* he says it provides '…the best steaks in the Dales'.

Skipton is quite firmly the capital of Craven. Everything and everybody flocks there - whether by road, rail or canal - and there is a pub for every taste. The Red Lion in the high street dates from 1205 and not only is it the oldest pub in the town but one of the oldest buildings in Craven. The most historic is the Black Horse opposite, a listed building whose coaching arch indicating one of its former purposes. Much of it is seventeenth century, but it is on the site of the Royal Mews of Richard III when he was Lord of the Honour of Skipton between 1483 and 1485. The Georgian three-storied Devonshire Hotel has a notable eighteenth century staircase and some other fine decor, including panelled window shutters. The Castle Inn and the Craven Hotel are both early nineteenth century town pubs, whilst the Albion from the same period was a coaching inn despite its locked-in situation in a side street. The Royal Oak also serviced the coaches. The Midland is a fine Victorian railway hotel lying opposite the station whereas the Station, a Victorian end-of-terrace boozer, is for some reason more than a mile away.

At Embsay the eighteenth century Elm Tree stands in the shade of a large tree on the village green, assumed to be an elm although it may well be a hornbeam. There are mounting steps at the front for horsemen. The Bay Horse, which is now a bank, had a bull-baiting ring in the forecourt.

The imposing White Lion at Kildwick-in-Craven is seventeenth century; it has been a coaching and posting house with stables, and in later days continued to serve as a post office.

When Richard Laycock was the landlord of the Bay Horse at Sutton-in-Craven in 1850 he used to brew his own beer, using Clough Beck, which ran alongside the pub, to keep his barrels cool in hot weather. The pub dates from before 1822. The small, stone-built Kings Arms, built towards the end of the nineteenth century, was the headquarters of a sick club for which the subscription was sixpence a week. The benefits were ten shillings a week when off sick for up to two months and then five shillings for another four weeks; and there was a shareout of profits at Christmas. At nearby Glusburn the Dog and Gun — which became a pub around 1850 — was formerly a farm in the longhouse style that had been mentioned in the *Domesday Book*.

A Band of Hope was formed in Sutton in 1863 which lasted for twenty years, giving way to a Temperance Society which had its own drum and fife band. They paraded the village with their own song to the tune of *John Peel*:

> 'In beer there's a poison, yes it's true,
> In whisky and cider and cocktails too,
> Leave them alone its the best thing to do,
> Or you'll ne'er be a total abstainer.'

There is evidence of a hostelry in Keighley as far back as the fourteenth century. It is said that the Fleece was the oldest inn in the town, but that is long since closed and the Lord Rodney is probably the oldest surviving one. Its name, however, dates from no earlier than 1782 when the barony was created, Admiral Sir George Rodney having taken part in the victory at Cape St Vincent and being ennobled shortly afterwards. It has the date 1692 on its windows and there is a record in the register of St Andrews Church of a visit by Archbishop John Sharp of York who: '...visited Ye Red Lion by the church gates'. He reigned at York from 1691 to 1714, so the date seems to be correct.

Up to 1960 a number of licensed houses in Keighley were genuine alehouses and could not sell wines and spirits. Some, like the Brown Cow, dated from the 1830 Beerhouse Act. In that year it was converted from three cottages and has changed little in style since then. The Eastwood Tavern went beyond 1960 before ceasing to be an alehouse (it was the last one in the town). Its conversion came out of four back-to-back cottages — evidence of this remains with its room layout and the two flights of stairs in the cellar that lead nowhere. There is supposed to be a pub ghost but it has not been seen for years.

In the period that rugby league football was being created, clubs used various inducements to attract players. Keighley Rugby Club used the Black Horse in Market Street to lodge their players, and it was claimed that the fact that it had a billiard hall attached was an illegal inducement. One player who stayed there was Harry Myers who became the club captain and later had his own pub. This was the Worth Valley Hotel at Ingrow which is now called the Worth Valley Inn, a subtle difference made even more confusing by the fact that when the present Worth Valley Inn was called the Worth Valley Hotel, the Great Northern Hotel (also in Ingrow) was called the Worth Valley Inn!

The most enduring character in the life of Keighley's taverns in the nineteenth century was Henry Hargreaves Thompson — also known as 'Henry Tap' — who was born at Colne in 1823. He became the ostler at the Crown Inn in Keighley, and later the tapster (manager) of the Fleece Tap which stood behind the Fleece Inn in Low Street. He was landlord of the Black Bull in Old Bridge Street when its name was changed to the Royal Oak, and he advertised the fact in the *Keighley News,* also pointing out that he was a dealer in furniture and clocks and ran a pig market! When the Royal Oak closed in 1869 the

Branwell Brontë's chair used to be at the Black Bull in Haworth.

pig market continued. He was brewing at the White Horse in 1865 and later owned the Malt Shovel.

The Brontë family dominate the town of Haworth, and most of the older pubs claim Branwell as a former regular. They may all be correct, for he died an alcoholic. The Fleece was one of his haunts, although John Wesley was there before him at this sixteenth century coaching house. He held meetings in the upper room and preached for William Grimshaw, Rector of Haworth. This was the post Patrick Brontë was to take up in 1820. Branwell is said to have favoured the Black Bull above all others in the town, possibly because it is near to the parsonage. His chair was exhibited here for many years, but with the increase in popularity of Brontë memorabilia it was sold.

The Kings Arms is one of the oldest buildings in the town and in 1600 was the courthouse; and the Old White Lion is more than 300 years old. It is difficult to escape the Brontës here: the Toby Jug — now a restaurant — is allegedly haunted by the ghost of Emily on the anniversary of her death, the 19th December. (There have been no recent manifestations.) There was also a ghost at the Sun but when a landlord placed a gargoyle over the door it disappeared.

The best known of the area's haunted pubs is the Old Silent at Stanbury. Its name stems from the fact that Bonnie Prince Charlie was hidden here — a trapdoor remains through which he escaped — and the locals kept silent for four weeks to allow him to get away. Its ghost is that of a former landlady who strokes the heads of sleeping visitors. She used to ring a bell to bring in stray cats from the moors for food. The bells can be heard to this day, and there are still many cats around the place. Halliwell Sutcliffe, who wrote much on Yorkshire, set his novel *Rycroft of Withens* here.

CLARO

'The situation of High Harrowgate is exceedingly pleasant, and commands a most extensive prospect of the distant country, finely varied by towns, villages, fields and woods.'
E Hargrove

There are at least ten pubs in Yorkshire called the Craven Heifer, but the one in Addingham has the distinction of being nearest to where the 308 stone beast was born at Bolton Abbey in 1807. This long straggling village on the main road from Ilkley to Skipton has a fair share of pubs, with the Sailor being its most unusually named one. Addingham couldn't be farther from the sea, but here at one time was the headquarters of a seafarers' employment agency. The Crown is a village roadside inn dating from 1759; and the Swan — with its four rooms and a stand-up area — has a ghost which may well be one of the former occupants of a now unused room that was originally the village mortuary.

There have been inns and taverns in Ilkley since the Middle Ages. Possibly the earliest record is, quite appositely, in the 1379 Poll Tax returns where reference is made to one Henry Spenser, a hostiler. But there are few more details available until the beginning of the nineteenth century when, in an 1822 directory, the Rose and Crown and the Wheatsheaf are mentioned. Both, though, were thought to be very old. Later the Rose and Crown was rebuilt and it carried on its business along with that of a barber's shop. The present building in Church Street still retains the rebuilt stone facade.

These two inns were joined in 1825 by the Listers Arms, the oldest surviving licensed premises in Ilkley. It is now a large residential hotel, but it is quite likely that it was expanded from its original days when it was referred to as the New Inn. It takes its present name from its first tenant, John Lister. Ilkley had just these three inns for another thirty years, although there are odd records of beerhouses opening and closing (a not unusual occurence after Wellington's Act of 1830 allowed any householder to buy a licence).

But in the 1850's, responding to the popularity of the town as a spa and health resort, more were to open. The Star was one, although the present building, which sports a superb clock next to its front door from the former Hammonds Brewery of Bradford, dates from a complete rebuild in 1905. The Cow and Calf in Ben Rhydding was another, and they were followed by the Station in 1861. Whilst this was demolished in 1880 to make way for an extension of the railway line to Skipton, it was replaced by the Midland Hotel, named after the railway company.

The Albion, built in 1870, had a short life but apparently a merry one. One room was available for 'pick-nick' parties; it also housed 'assembly rooms' and had a iron water spring. The Middelton Hotel opened in 1876 and later changed its name to the Ilkley Moor Hotel. Sadly it was destroyed by fire in 1968 but the 'taps', or public bar, survived.

The 'taps' is all that remains of the Ilkley Moor Hotel.

208

The Hermit at Burley Woodhead recalls Job Senior, born in Ilkley in 1780 and blessed with the power to sing treble, alto, tenor and bass within the same hymn. He was left a fortune, squandered it on drink and shortly after marrying late in life had the misfortune to lose his wife in a domestic accident, for which was unjustly blamed. His wife's relatives destroyed his house and stole his savings. He turned hermit and lived at Burley Woodhead on the edge of Ilkley Moor. He became a prophet on the weather and was thought to possess the power to foresee the future. One day when feeling unwell some youths added spirits to his ale and it made him worse. He had cholera and he died in a barn by the Wheatsheaf Inn on the Ilkley Road. He was seventy-seven and is buried in the churchyard at Burley-in-Wharfedale.

At one time, walkers heading for the Timble Inn in Washburndale would find it by following an intriguing series of signposts: 'Timble Inn — 5 miles'; 'Timble Inn — straight on'; 'Timble Inn — 10 minutes'; and final one that proclaimed:

> 'Call at the Timble Inn
> 5 minutes walk
> Fine Ales
> Good Catering'

And according to Alfred J Brown, who wrote well of walking in the county, they would find just that. Even today its description in *North Yorkshire Ale* says it is popular with hikers and fishermen and has no jukebox.

Further up the valley at Thruscross is the 400 year old Stonehouse Inn with its original carved wood fireplace. It looks over the reservoir which covers the one-time village of West End. Also there was the Gate Inn, a beerhouse where the sign read:

> 'The gate hangs well and hinders none,
> Drink hearty boys and travel on.'

Although some sources claim that the final line read:

> 'Refresh yourself, and pay, and travel on.'

In 1789 the Honourable John Byng, in his *Torrington Diaries,* compared the journey of an unknown traveller in Yorkshire some 200 years previously with what he calls the insolence and blasphemy of modern inns (that is, eighteenth century inns):

'In my last return from Edenborough in Scotland, coming homeword through Yorkshire, I traveled somewhat out of the common high ...I chanced to come to a little thorough fare town, call'd Rippon, where, at the very ent'ring into the town I met a poore old woman, of whom I asked if there were any good lodging in the town: she answered me that there was lodging at the Signe of the Great Omega — And thither I went and ent'ring into the house, I found in the hall, the goodman, his two sonnes, his chamberlain and his hostler singing the CIIII [104th] Psalme of David very distinctly and orderly; the goodwife with her two daughters sat spinning at their wheeles a little distance from them.

So I bad them God speed. The hoste very curteously arose, and bad me welcome: so did the wife also, and asked me whether I meant to tarry all night, I answered yea. — Then he asked me if I would see my chamber. No, gentle hoste, (quoth I,) I will not hinder so much your good exercise, for I am sure I cannot be lodged amisse in this house. Not so, sir (quoth he) but ye shall have the best that we hav, and welcome. I gave him hasty thanks. Then he enwuir'd of mee, of whence I was, where I had been, and whether I was bound. I told him I was a southern man borne and dwelling, and that I had been at Edenborough in Scotland: and was thus farre in my way homeward. In good time, sir, (quoth he,) and yee are hartely welcome into this part of Yorkshire. I thank ye, gentle hoste, (quoth I) &c. &c.'

Ripon had other attractions in the olden days. At the Unicorn in the market place there was a servant called Thomas Spence during the latter part of the eighteenth century. He would welcome guests with a boot jack and a pair of slippers, and was known affectionately as 'Old Boots'. Spence had no teeth and he would accept the coins he was tipped with between his chin and his nose and then bow his thanks. He was the last person to be buried in the Minster yard.

The Unicorn stands next to the town hall where a horn is blown

Thomas Spence — 'Old Boots' — from the Unicorn at Ripon.

each evening. The city's motto is 'Except the Lord keep the city the wakeman waketh in vain' and the town hall was the wakeman's house. Together with the aldermen he had responsibility for the safety of Ripon from 9 pm, when the horn was blown, until sunrise.

Yet another inn named after a champion racehorse can be found at Summerbridge. The Flying Dutchman fulfilled its great potential as a two year old when it won the Champagne Stakes by achieving the remarkable double of winning the Derby and the St Leger in 1849. (There is another similarly-named pub at Wombwell near Barnsley, and at one time there was one in York.) Near to Harrogate, the Little Wonder remembers the Derby winner of 1840, a remarkable horse that was only fifteen hands high, cost its owner just sixty-five guineas and won at the amazing odds of fifty to one.

There is no pub at present in Ripley, although moves are afoot to reopen Star House as one. It was formerly the Star Inn, but was closed down by Sir William Ingleby in 1919 because he disapproved of worshippers leaving Ripley Church opposite and heading straight for the inn. It was a coaching inn, the first stop on an express service that ran between Leeds and Edinburgh.

If ever there was a unique name for an inn it was the one in Nidd called Ass in the Band-Box. It was built in 1712 and is thought to have had an original coat of arms with a unicorn (ass) inside a crown (band-box). The sign was repainted in 1800 when the figure became Napoleon sitting on an ass sailing in a band-box to invade England. (What may appear preposterous and jingoistic nonsense was extremely popular in those days.) But later the pub acquired the nickname of 'My Arse in a Band-Box'!

In 1687 the first inn for spa visitors was opened in Harrogate and the eighteenth century saw an expansion in the development of the town. It was noted that in 1818 there were '...nine inns in High and Low Harrogate...' and all of these would provide accomodation. Some of these, like the Granby, the Crown and the Swan have developed into fashionable hotels. Another was the Queens Head which was described as an '...inn that dines with ease 120 with 50 servants attending.'

There were, of course, taverns with no accomodation and the fashionable Hales Bar was an early example of a gin palace. It is 200 years old and situated close to the Pump Room. It remains gas-lit with some original glass work and panelling. There are two sulphur wells

Hales Bar in Harrogate was formerly known as the Promenade Inn.

in the cellar. The County, which fronts on to part of the town's famous Stray, is a listed building dating from 1830 and the North Eastern, which faces the railway station from which its name derives, is Victorian with Edwardian touches.

Mother Shipton is Knaresborough's most famous personage. She was a witch and the pub that bears her name also records her birth on its sign: 'Near this Petrifying Well I first drew breath as records tell.' The pub is at the entrance to the dropping well, the witch's cave and other attractions of this fine town. It is a seventeenth century building and contains some ancient relics, but has only been a pub since the nineteenth century. The sign also shows Mother Shipton outside the cave with her black cat. She was born Ursula Southiel in 1488 and a contemporary description of her is not flattering:

'...[she had a] nose of incredible and unproportionate length, having many crooks and turnings adorned with strange pimples of diverse colours...'

Despite this, she was wed by Tobias Shipton and they lived in the town where she plied her trade as a prophetess. Her most famous prophecy was that Cardinal Wolsey would not become Archbishop of York. When he reached Cawood he was arrested for high treason, and he died on the journey back to London. She also predicted:

'The world to an end shall come,

In eighteen hundred and eighty-one.'

It is assumed that the Worlds End public house is named after this false prophecy, although other claims are that there are several similarly-named houses which are near the end of a town, like this one. However at one time the sign showed an earthquake with a bus falling into a river.

Another of Knaresborough's historic characters was Eugene Aram, and an inn once called the White Horse took his name. Aram was a teacher who had his school in White Horse Yard during the eighteenth century. He was convicted of the murder of Daniel Clark fourteen years after the man's supposed death, and hung at York. Many people had doubts about Aram's culpability and his conviction is regarded as a cause célèbre in Knaresborough.

The Borough Bailiff in High Street was the residence of that luminary during the seventeenth century, although the exterior was replaced during the eighteenth. The Old Royal Oak in Market Place is also seventeenth century. In 1823 the Crown in High Street was listed as the town's principal coaching house and commercial inn. And the little elephant has the unique distinction of being spelled officially in only lower case letters.

THE PRAISE OF YORKSHIRE ALE

'O Yorkshire, Yorkshire: Thy Ale is so strong,
That it will kill us all if we stay long:
So they agreed a Journey for to make
Into the South, some Respit there to take.'

The Praise of Yorkshire Ale, George Meriton *1684*

When Meriton wrote his *The Praise of Yorkshire Ale* it was the day of the ale-wife when women did the brewing, and he mentions two in his epic poem, Madam Bradley of Northallerton and Nanny Driffield of Easingwold. It was the day of the ale-conner when ale would be poured on to a wooden seat and a man in leather trousers would sit on it to test its strength. If the seat came with him when he stood up, it passed. It was the day of 'humming' ale, so called presumably because the tight, creamy head on ale so beloved of Yorkshiremen to this day was said to hum. Of Stingo, which became so famous that as far away as Marylebone there was a pub called the Yorkshire Stingo; of Knockerdown and Rumtum. And it was the day when by law ale cost one penny a quart.

The Old Brewery in Tadcaster — now run by the Samuel Smith company — is the oldest in Yorkshire still operating, dating from 1758. But brewing in Yorkshire, if not timeless, can count back at least 2,000 years to Roman days. In ancient times, inns, taverns and alehouses would brew their own beer, and it was not until the seventeenth century that the common brewer emerged; that is to say a brewer who would supply anyone, be they alehouse, farmhouse or private house.

The earliest established common brewers in Yorkshire were the Nesfield family of Scarborough who started in 1691. They were in business until taken over by Moors and Robsons Breweries of Hull in 1919, but continued brewing until 1932. Tadcaster, which occasionally calls itself with some justification the 'Burton of the

North', has recorded brewhouses in the town from as early as 1341. The Old Brewery was founded in 1758 by John and William Hartley, traded originally as Hartley and Son and later as Hartley and Backhouse, until it was sold to John Smith in 1847.

The Smiths are just one of the great brewing families of Yorkshire, but together with Taylor, Tetley, Stones and Webster are the only ones still identified in today's brewing scene. Gone are the Bentleys, Hammond, Ramsden, the Seniors, Whitaker of Bradford and Whitaker of Halifax and many others. They flourished in the nineteenth century when production — and presumably demand — was many times that of today. As beers were relatively cheap they were also regarded as food which resulted in the high consumption figures.

Craftsmanship in a former William Whitaker pub.

A word of clarification here may help. During the nineteenth century, beer was much stronger in terms of original gravity (OG) than it is today. The term is related to the amount of fermentable materials at the beginning of any brew and is the standard by which excise duty is reckoned. An original gravity of 1040 would indicate that forty parts of fermentable matter such as malt and sugar have been added to 1,000 parts of water, or liquor as the brewers call it. It is not an absolute measure of strength, but a good indication. The alcoholic strength of beer depends also on the gravity level to which the beer is allowed to ferment down to, or to attenuate. It could reach 1000 and all the fermentables would have been converted into alcohol.

Today's brewing techniques are more sophisticated than a century and more ago, when beers started at much higher gravities but their attenuation was probably limited and they finished up as low in alcohol and very sweet. An indication of the differences in original gravity can be seen from the average given of all the beers brewed by Joshua Tetley in 1850, which was 1073, and the national average in 1982 of 1037. Tetley's strongest beer in 1850 was called Imperial; it had an original gravity of 1097. Imperial today has an original gravity of 1042.

Timothy Bentley started production in his brewery at Lockwood near Huddersfield in 1795, although he was known to have brewed on a much smaller basis in Calderdale for some years previously, probably as a home brewer. In 1830 he went into partnership with William Shaw and the firm prospered into the Victorian era, the brewery being rebuilt in 1868. But Bentley is best known for his invention of the Yorkshire Stone Square method of fermentation. In fairness the credit must be shared with Edward Riley who patented the system in 1830. Bentley's method involved a double chamber with the top section divided from the rest to prevent the yeast from returning to the brewing liquid. The originals were made of stone slabs, and some firms claimed they affected the taste and quality of the ale by giving it more flavour and a fullness not found with other methods. Nowadays the stone has been replaced by stainless steel but the system is still used, particularly in Yorkshire breweries.

Bentley and Shaw went public in 1891 and took over Benjamin Ainley's Royd Steam Brewery at Lindley in 1927. In 1936 it won a silver medal at the Brewery Exhibition for its Town Ale, and by the start of the Second World War the firm owned more than 200 public houses. However in 1944 the Bradford firm of Hammonds took them over and they are now part of the Bass empire. The brewery at Lockwood remains, but brewing ceased there years ago and is now a depot and offices for the present owners.

Bentley's son, Henry, built the Eshaldwell Brewery at Woodlesford in 1828, although there had been brewing on the site for nearly sixty years. In 1892 the firm of Henry Bentley and Company amalgamated

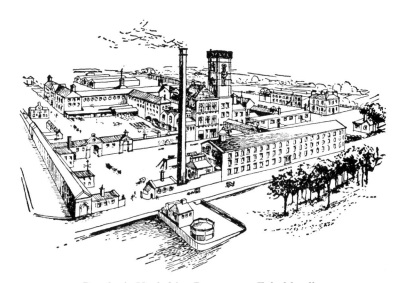

Bentley's Yorkshire Brewery at Eshaldwell.

with four others to form Bentley's Yorkshire Breweries Ltd — a strange plurality, for all the breweries except Woodlesford were closed down. A number of other companies were later taken over, including Scotts of Skipton in 1912 and Carters of Knottingley in 1935, and by 1962 the firm owned 420 pubs. Six years later they were to fall victim to the takeover fever that had gripped Britain, being bought out by Whitbreads. The brewery remains (it is now a listed building) but no brewing has taken place there since 1970.

Another branch of the Bentley family established a brewery in Rotherham in 1820. Bentleys Old Brewery (Rotherham) Ltd stayed in business until 1956 when it was taken over by Hammonds of Bradford. Robert Bentley, the founder and nephew of Timothy, also

218

Joshua Tetley, 1778-1859.

started another brewery at Ashton-under-Lyne in 1832 along with his
uncle's partner, William Shaw.

In 1822, Joshua Tetley took over a well-established brewery at
Salem Place, Leeds, from William Sykes who had brewed there for
thirty years. Tetley was a maltster and wine merchant, and at the age
of forty-four it may be thought that he was taking a chance in entering
another business. However it seemed to work and the full story can
be read in Clifford Lackey's excellent book *Quality Pays*. In Joshua
Tetley's lifetime the firm did not acquire any public houses; it was
1890 before they started to build up a tied estate. But when he died
in 1859 not only had the brewery been rebuilt but there were branch
offices in London, Dublin, Liverpool, Manchester and Birmingham.

The company was incorporated in 1897 but the Tetley family remained in control until 1960. (They were involved in public life, with two Lord Mayors of Leeds coming from the family.) Development continued gradually until 1954, when the purchase of Duncan Gilmour and Company with its 342 pubs gave Tetleys a firm foothold in Sheffield and South Yorkshire. William Whitaker of Bradford followed in 1959, although Tetleys had been supplying their 127 pubs with beer since 1928. In 1960 the Melbourne Brewery of Leeds with 245 pubs was bought for £3.5 million. Melbourne had purchased the Russell and Wrangham Company of Malton only two years before, and in 1961 Tetleys sold it again with its ninety public houses to Camerons of Hartlepool.

In 1960 Tetley and the Liverpool-based firm of Walker Cain decided to amalgamate to form Tetley Walker. Between them they owned 2,771 pubs, with breweries in Leeds and Warrington. And, in the following year, Tetley Walker got together with Ind Coope of Burton-upon-Trent and Ansells of Birmingham to form Allied Breweries, now Allied Lyons plc. The takeovers continued, however, and the Leeds brewery acquired the 204 houses of Thomas Ramsden and Son of Halifax and 65 from Charles Rose and Son of Malton. Nowadays the trading companies are split by the Pennines, and the Leeds company controls 1,100 pubs in Yorkshire, the North East and the East Midlands.

Unlike Joshua Tetley, Samuel Webster entered the brewing business at the comparatively early age of twenty-five when he bought the Fountain Head Brewery at Ovenden Wood near Halifax in 1838. He had been a butcher in Mount Pellon and had no previous experience in the trade, but he was to start a tied estate much earlier than Tetley by buying the Lane Ends Inn at Wheatley in 1845. More followed and by 1880 the firm owned 100 pubs. Three of his four sons were to follow him into the business, so the company took the name of Samuel Webster and Sons.

The firm were soon into the business of acquiring other companies, and in 1878 bought the Albert Springs Brewery at Boothtown and thirteen houses from John Sykes for £22,000. Others followed in the present century, including the Shibden Head Brewery in 1933, the Wappy Springs Brewery at Outlane in 1957, Daniel Fielding's White Castle Brewery at Bradshaw in 1961, and finally J Hey and Company of Bradford with their seventy-five pubs in 1966. Websters were to fall into the hands of the Grand Metropolitan empire in 1972 and are now amalgamated with Wilsons of Manchester, whose brewery has been closed.

Seth Senior started brewing at the Sovereign Inn at Shepley in 1829. He later built the Highfield Brewery and bought the St Marks Brewery in the town. He also owned a colliery at Kirkburton which supplied coal to his own private gas works. Two of his sons, Reuben and James, worked with him and saw the firm develop — by 1895 they were brewing 1,000 barrels of beer in a week. In 1946 the firm with its ninety-nine licensed houses was taken over by Hammonds of Bradford, and the following year the brewery was closed.

Two other sons, Paul and Guy Senior, went off to seek their own fortune and in 1861 established a brewery in Barnsley. They maintained the business at the Oakwell Brewery until 1888 when it was acquired by the newly formed Barnsley Brewery Company, and by the turn of the century it owned 100 public houses. There were several takeovers between the wars and in the 1940's, but by 1957 the Tadcaster brewers John Smiths had an interest in the company and took control of it in 1961. Brewing continued at Oakwell until 1975 and then the much-loved Barnsley Bitter was no more.

The Smiths of Tadcaster saga is a simple one, but often mistold. It started in 1847 when John Smith bought the brewery of Hartley and Backhouse, which he ran until he died in 1879. He left the business to his two sons, Samuel and William, but a family row broke out which was not resolved until William built the 'new' brewery and continued the firm in his father's name. Samuel kept the original — the 'old' brewery which is incorporated in the firm's title — and the relationship of the two companies became nothing more than next door neighbours.

Samuel Smith ran his firm until he died in 1927 when it passed to his son. When he died in 1964, control moved to his sons, Humphrey and Oliver Smith, who are still there. There have been some relatively small takeovers, with McQuats of Leeds in 1947 and the Rochdale and Manor Brewery in 1948 being the most important. It remains a fiercely independent brewing company, the largest in Yorkshire outside of the so-called 'big six' companies.

The pattern created by Tetley and Webster was to be followed by William Smith. He was quickly into the takeover business, and before the turn of the century he had acquired breweries in Driffield, Thirsk and Market Weighton. Ten more were to follow, of which the most significant were Warwick and Company of Boroughbridge in 1924, Whitworth of Wath-upon-Dearne in 1958, Barnsley in 1961 and Warwick and Richardsons of Newark in 1962. Then it was to lose its own independence and become part of the Courage empire in 1970, and later that company's successor, Imperial Group. When that firm fell to the Hanson Trust, most of the brewing divison was sold off to the Australian predator, Elders.

Sheffield had more than thirty breweries in the late nineteenth century, including some of the most important in Yorkshire. Today, sadly, no independent ones remain. Edward and Robert Tennant built up an empire that at its height amounted to 700 pubs but it was then, in 1962, that it was plucked by Whitbread. The Exchange Brewery dates from 1840 and is still in business. Tennant Brothers took over several breweries, including the Worksop and Retford Company in 1959 with its estate of 192 pubs.

William Stones moved to the Cannon Brewery in the Neepsend area of Sheffield in 1860, and although the firm is now part of the Bass group it still trades under its own name, an indication of how some major brewers protect what are established brand names. Stones absorbed the Mappins Masboro Old Brewery of Rotherham with its 100 pubs in 1954.

In 1892 Christopher Carter, Eleazar Milner and George Bird formed a company which started brewing at the Hope Brewery, and in 1940 the company amalgamated with Henry Tomlinson and Company after that firm's Anchor Brewery was demolished during an air raid. They brewed mainly bottle beers and were best known for

Jubilee Stout, which continues in production today by the Bass group that took them over in 1962.

Septimus Henry Ward injected capital into an established brewing company, changed its location and named it after himself; it went on to become one of Sheffield's best-known breweries. Wards is still brewing today at the Sheaf Brewery, but the company was taken over by Vaux of Sunderland in 1972.

Vaux also took over W M Darley of Thorne, which had been established since the mid-nineteenth century. It remained in family control until the acquisition in 1978 but continued to brew for another eight years. When the brewery closed in 1986, the firm's eighty-eight houses were still supplied with Darley beers brewed by Wards in Sheffield.

T & R Theakston of Masham has remained a family-run business from its start in 1827, although it has been taken over twice, firstly by Matthew Brown of Blackburn in 1984 and again when that firm fell to Scottish and Newcastle Breweries three years later. There are still members of the family in this firm, which is noted for its oddly-spelled Old Peculier beer, named after an ecclesiastic dignitary.

Timothy Taylor's brewery in Keighley remains — like Samuel Smith's — firmly in family control and in robust independence. The firm was established in 1858 and moved house five years later to their present site, selling the old brewery to another company. The Knowle Spring Brewery was extended in 1911, and trade to their small estate and the free trade was restricted to a manageable distance from the brewery. The only approach to a takeover came in 1966 when they bought seven pubs belonging to Parkers of Haworth when that firm went into liquidation. The present chairman and managing director, Lord Ingrow, is the grandson of the founder.

Hull ale has been praised by famous men, John Taylor the water poet and Samuel Pepys to name but two. John Ward started a brewery in 1765 in Dagger Lane, the forerunner of the Hull Brewery Company. It moved to bigger premises in Silvester Street in 1868. In 1972 it became part of Northern Dairies and traded as North Country Breweries, until a takeover by the Mansfield Brewery in 1985, who

Timothy Taylor's Knowle Spring Brewery at Ingrow.

closed it down but continued to run the 200 pubs.

The city's other well-known brewery, Moors and Robsons, came about as a result of a merger in 1888 and was originally known as Hull United Breweries. In 1919 it took over Nesfields of Scarborough and Guy and Company of Grimsby, and in 1960 the brewery and 138 houses were acquired by Hewitt Brothers of Grimsby.

John J Hunt founded his Ebor Brewery in York in 1834, a popular time to latch on to the trade provided by the vast increase in the number of beerhouses needing supplies as a result of the 1830 Beer-house Act. The firm took over Brogdens of Tockwith in 1904 and the Scarborough and Whitby Breweries in 1934. But Camerons of Hartlepool gradually moved in on Hunts and, after taking a controlling interest, acquired it completely in 1955.

York also housed the Yorkshire Clubs Brewery at Huntingdon from 1934 until it became part of the Northern Clubs Federation Brewery in 1975. This unique organisation supplied mainly to working men's clubs, who were the company's shareholders.

James Hammond bought the Fountain Brewery in Bradford in 1860 from Joseph Pullan, who had built it twenty years before. Its development in the inter-war years was rapid, acquiring brewery companies in Ilkley, Heckmondwike, Bingley and Wakefield. From 1945 this continued apace, with a name change the following year to Hammonds United Breweries following the acquisiton of the Tadcaster Tower Brewery. Brewing ceased at Bradford in 1955 but the company had four production units at Huddersfield, Barrow, Edinburgh and Tadcaster. More takeovers followed in Yorkshire and Lancashire, but by 1960 the wheel on which H U B rotated had turned full circle; they became part of Northern Breweries of Great Britain, who merged with Charringtons to form Charringtons United Breweries, later Bass Charrington and now simply Bass.

Kirkstall Brewery in Leeds was built in 1834 by Thomas Walker, who sold it to Benjamin Dawson in 1845. Like Tetley the firm resisted moving into the tied estate and concentrated on the free trade. It had a London office when the Kirkstall Brewery Company took over from Dawson in 1871. It had an extensive export trade and used two steamships to move beer along the navigations to the docks at Hull. Only in 1895 did it start to buy licensed properties, and soon built up a substantial chain. It became part of the Blackburn brewers Duttons in 1936, who continued to brew there until 1966. By this time Whitbreads owned Duttons and they carried on brewing until 1984.

Few people remember Leeds and Wakefield Breweries Ltd, but mention Melbourne in Leeds and most people aged fifty and above will recall it at once. The Melbourne Brewery was in Regent Street from 1846 under the control of Kirk Matthews and Company. In 1889 an amalgamation with Carter and Company of the Victoria Brewery in Wakefield brought the new title. This was to remain until 1958 when Russell and Wrangham of Malton was bought and the name changed to Melbourne Breweries Ltd. Wallers of Bradford had been the only other takeover in 1935, but the company had been aggressive in their acquisition policy and purchased many individual pubs. The brewery and 245 houses fell to Tetleys just two years after it became Melbourne.

There have, of course, been many others. Towards the end of the nineteenth century there were probably 250 common brewers in Yorkshire. Some remain as memories among older folk, such as Hepworths of Ripon, Clarksons of Barnsley, Richard Whitaker of Halifax and Hemingway of Leeds, whilst others are long gone and can only be found in the records.

But there are also new breweries, a phenomenon that would not have been believed twenty years ago when the cult was to shut down all but the big production companies. Takeovers were about pubs and outlets, and breweries went to the wall. However, Frankins of Harrogate, Trough of Bradford, Old Mill of Snaith and several others have started up in the last few years, along with the return to brewing of companies like the Selby Brewery and Clarks of Wakefield. These changes have come about following the success of CAMRA, the Campaign for Real Ale, which was formed in 1971. Michael Young, who founded the Consumers' Association, described it as '...the most successful campaigning organisation in Europe'. But that is another story.

THE ROOMS OF A PUB

At least thirty-five different names for the various rooms of a public house have been found in the researching for this book. Some are unique — for example the Bagatelle Room in the White Lion at Sheffield — whilst others like the lounge, tap room and public bar are very common. The derivation and purpose of some of these rooms are given below:

Assembly room/hall: mainly from the eighteenth century; a large room used for balls, dinners and public meetings.

Bar: a room with service and not necessarily one with a servery (also called a bar) in it. There are several different types of bars.

Best room: originally called the parlour and now called the lounge, but meaning exactly what it says.

Buffet: a refreshment room where food can usually be obtained. Often found in Teesside pubs and other parts of the North East.

Buttery: strictly speaking, a storeroom for bottles — from the French *bouteille* — but used to indicate a room where drinks are served through a buttery-hatch.

Club room: a room, usually upstairs, used for meetings of various organisations such as Oddfellows and Freemasons.

Cocktail bar: little-used these days except in hotels, but meaning exactly what it says; a bar where cocktails are served.

Coffee (or tea) room: created in the nineteenth century in opposition to temperance coffee houses. They often provided newspapers.

Concert room: similar to the assembly room, but more working-class and used as opposition to working men's clubs.

Family room: a modern innovation, where children are allowed in but in which there is no direct access to a servery for alcohol.

Four ale bar: rarely seen these days, but intended originally for the sale of beers — ale, bitter, old and porter.

Games room: an alternative name for the tap room or vault, in which darts, dominoes and other games are played. The modern version is the pool room.

Ladies (only) room: exactly what it says. A late nineteenth century innovation but now illegal.

Lounge: introduced in the 1930's from ships and hotels. Usually the best room, and may be the only carpeted one.

Lounge bar: same as a lounge, except where there are both, in which case the use is pretentious and it is really a tap room or vault.

Men's bar: 'men only' bars, once commonplace but now illegal.

Parlour: derived from the development of the private house into the public house, and is the best room.

Private bar: usually small rather than private, and may also be called the snug or the select.

Public bar: formerly the kitchen and also known as the tap room or vault. The pub's equivalent of a third-class railway carriage.

Saloon bar: originally the middle bar, but as the number of rooms decreased it became the lounge, although it is still in common use.

Smoke room: a classless room introduced after cigarettes became popular in the nineteenth century, even though smoking was allowed in others. Non-smoking rooms and areas are a recent innovation.

Snug: another name for the private bar.

Tap room: where casks are 'tapped', and often called a vault or vaults. Both refer to the cellar or store. The predecessor of the public bar.

METHODS OF DISPENSING

In the same way as cask-conditioned beer is these days a unique British institution, then so is the traditional method of dispense by the handpump. And credit for the invention must go to a Yorkshireman, Joseph Bramah, who was born at Stainborough near Barnsley in 1748.

Until then, beer had been served by gravity direct from the cask in the tap room of the pub. The need for better quality brought about the use of cool cellars in which casks were racked, and the landlord or potboys would draw off the beer into large jugs, return to the bar and then pour it into the glass or tankard. This was time-consuming and expensive.

For years pumps had been used to draw water from wells and keep ships afloat, yet no-one seems to have thought of a similar system for serving beer — until Joseph Bramah. He was a prolific inventor, but his patent taken out in 1797 for a 'beer engine' showed a cumbersome machine involving the re-racking of beer and the use of boxes of sand. Three years later Thomas Parkinson patented what he called '...an hydrostatic engine or machine for the purpose of drawing beer or any other liquors out of a cellar or vault in a public house'. Others followed, and the use of 'beer engines' with hand pumps soon became the vogue.

The system was modified and more sophisticated types were introduced, including a 'cash register' with three or four handles mounted on the bar. These remained popular until the 1930's, and one is still in use at the Eagle at Skerne in the East Riding. The lead piping which linked the cask with the pump soon became unpopular on health grounds, and today plastic pipes are universal.

The introduction of electric motors to replace the handpump came about in the 1930's. There are two methods: the 'free flow' system which simply draws beer from the cask whilst switched on; and the metered pump which uses a diaphragm to measure a pre-set amount, usually a half pint. The latter are popular in the Midlands and Manchester area, but are seldom seen in Yorkshire except around Sheffield, where some brewers use them to dispense both traditional and keg or 'bright' beers.

Electric pumps had some popularity along with keg beers in the 1960's and 1970's. Hand pumps had their renaissance when traditional beers came back into fashion as a result of the activities of the Campaign for Real Ale.

For the record, 'real' ale — often called 'traditional' or 'cask-conditioned' — is brewed from traditional ingredients, matured by secondary fermentation in the container from which it is to be dispensed, and served without the use of extraneous carbon dioxide (CO_2) pressure. This recognises that beer can be packaged in a cask or bottle and that CO_2 is an integral part of the drink.

INDEX OF BREWERIES

Numbers in italics refer to illustrations

232

INDEX OF LANDLORDS & PUB OWNERS

Numbers in italics refer to illustrations

INDEX OF PUBS

Numbers in italics refer to illustrations

240

GENERAL INDEX

Numbers in italics refer to illustrations

Harewood
  House 45
  Earl of 74
Hargrove, E 206
Harome 163
Harrogate 3, 7, 10, 46, 168, 185,
  211-212, 225
  Pump Room 211
  Stray 212
Hartlepool 219, 223
Hartley, John 23
Hartley, John and William 215
Hartoft End 172
Hartshead 97
  moor 97
Hastings, Lady Elizabeth (Betty)
  24
Hatfield 20
Hatfield Woodhouse 20
Hawke, Lord 54-5
Haworth 87, 205, 222
  parsonage 205
Hawthorne, Nathaniel 141
Headingley 59
Hebden Bridge 85
Heckmondwike 224
Hedon 124
  Haven Commissioners 124
Helmsley 161-2
Hempstead, Essex 127
Henry VII 75
Henry VIII 40, 69, 156, 178
Heritage Inns, Joshua Tetley 14, 22,
  28, 144
Herring, J F 17
Herriot, James 188
Hessle 129
Heywood, Lord 31
Hicks, Seymour 67
Highroyd Well 80
Hightown 98
Hipswell Moor 187
Hogarth William 9
Hogg, Charles 72
Hollym 124

Holme 101
Holme Valley Beadlers 101
Holmfirth 101-2
Hood, Robin 15, 20, 97, 107, 151
Horsforth 53, 102
Horton-in-Ribblesdale 197
Hotham family 131
Hotham, Sir John 120, 131
Hotten, John Camden 142
Hoyland Nether 115
Hubberholme 69, 199
  parish church 199
  Poor Pasture 199
Huddersfield 7, 91-5, 98, 100, 224
  Broad Canal 92
  canal society 91
  Castle Hill 95
  manor court 93
  Narrow Canal 91
  town hall 93
Hudson, George 177
Hull 5, 10, 20, 32, 76, 119-123, 134,
  141, 144, 167, 214, 222-3
  General Election (1713) 119
  Humber ferry 122
  mug houses 119
  Victoria Pier 122
Humber Bridge 129
Humber, River 5, 20, 124, 126, 129
Humberside, County of 130
Hunmanby 167
Hunslet 1, 2, 14, 42-4
  Coghlan's Forge 44
  Grange Flats 44
  library 44
Hunsworth 97
Hunt, John J 223
Huntingdon (York) 223
Huntsman, Benjamin 105
Hustler, John 63
Hutchinson John 148
Hutchinson, Tommy 159
Hutton-le-Hole 174
Hutton, Rev John 197

256

Tan Hill 187-8, 189
Taylor, John, the Water Poet 76, 119, 141, 222
Taylor, Sir John: see Ingrow, Lord
Tees, River 179
temperance movement 9, *9*, 65, 78, 85, 202
Tennent, Edward 221
Tennent, Robert 221
Tetley, Charles Francis 37
Tetley, Joshua 37, 218, *218*
The Good Old Days 37
Thirsk 151, 156, 158, 178, 221
    museum 153
Thomas, Robert 85
Thompson, Robert (Mousey) 161, 163
Thorne 20, 222
Thornton-in-Lonsdale 197
    St Oswalds Church 197
    Yordas Cave 197
Thornton-le-Dale 164
Thruscross 208
Tilly, Vesta 74
Tockwith 223
Todmorden 6, 85
Tollerton 160
Topcliffe Fair 158
Torrington, Viscount:
    see Byng, John
Townsley, Christopher 53
Townsley, Lord 198
Towton, Battle of 22
Triangle 86
Trinity House 123
Trollope, Anthony 127
Tunstall 187
Turner, James W R 184, 197
turnpike riots 3, 39, 66
turnpike roads 3, 5, 98
Turpin, Dick 15, 24, 31, 54, 126-7, 138
Tyersall 66
Tyler, Wat 31

Uppermill 91

Vanburgh, Sir John 142
Victoria, Queen 17, 51, 64, 74, 95, 117, 151, 180
Voysey, C F A 35

Wadsworth 86
Wainhouse, John E 78-9
Wainstalls 87
Wakefield 3, 28, 115, 224, 225
Waldendale 191
Wales, Prince of (Edward VII) 45
Wales, Prince of (George IV) 16, 190
Walker, Albert 50
Walker, Thomas 7, 224
Walkington 130
Walton 29
Walton Hall, near Wakefield 63
War of Independence, American 85
Ward, John 222
Ward, Septimus Henry 222
Warrington 219
Warton family 128
Washburndale 208
Wath, near Pateley Bridge 3
Wath-upon-Dearne 221
Weavers' Company 54
Webster, Samuel 219
Weldrake 9, 132
Wellington, Duke of 6, 7, 122
Welton 126
Wensleydale 189
Wentbridge 21
Wentworth 115
Wesley, John 61, 156, 205
Wessenden Head 90
West Burton 191
West End 208
West Witton 191
West Yorkshire County Council 48
Westerham, Kent 137
Wetherby 26-7, 46
    Great Fire of 27
Wharfedale 49, 191, 199
Wheatley 219